SECRETS OF GREAT INFLUENCERS

50 Rules of Persuasion and Influence

Steven Pearce

SECRETS OF
GREAT INFLUENCERS

50 Rules of Persuasion and Influence

Steven Pearce

JOHN
MURRAY
BUSINESS

First published in Great Britain in 2014 by John Murray Learning.
An Hachette UK company.

This edition published by John Murray Business in 2026
An imprint of John Murray Press

I

A CIP catalogue record for this title is available from the British Library

Trade Paperback ISBN 978 1 399 83121 5
ebook ISBN 978 1 399 83122 2

Typeset by KnowledgeWorks Global Ltd.

Printed and bound in Great Britain by Clays Ltd, Elcograf S.p.A.

John Murray Press policy is to use papers that are natural, renewable and recyclable products and made from wood grown in sustainable forests. The logging and manufacturing processes are expected to conform to the environmental regulations of the country of origin.

John Murray Press
Carmelite House
50 Victoria Embankment
London EC4Y 0DZ

John Murray Business
Hachette Book Group
123 South Broad Street
Ste 2750
Philadelphia, PA 19109, USA

www.johnmurraybusiness.com

John Murray Press, part of Hodder & Stoughton Limited
An Hachette UK company

The authorised representative in the EEA is Hachette Ireland, 8 Castlecourt Centre, Dublin 15, D15 XTP3, Ireland (email: info@hbgi.ie)

CONTENTS

Part 4: Who you are: influence through personal impact

Part 5: How you play the game: influence through politics

INTRODUCTION

- Are you paid the salary you deserve?
- Are your contributions in meetings given the attention they merit?
- Do you have the online following you would like?
- Are you 'in the know', part of the 'inner circle', a 'mover and a shaker'?

If the answer to any of these questions is no, then you are probably suffering from an influence deficit. Influence is the magic dust that gets things done and gets you where you want to go. Without it, life can seem like the punishment of Sisyphus: however much effort you put into rolling the boulder uphill, you seem condemned to watch it roll dispiritingly down to the bottom again.

This book will equip you with the strategies you need to take control of your life and achieve the results you are looking for. It will lift the lid on what it takes to be influential – the good, the bad and the sometimes ugly.

The views expressed in these pages are the result of more than ten years' work as a business consultant, during which time I have been privileged to observe the truly influential at close quarters around the world. The strategies I lay out I have mostly observed in action first hand, but I have also greatly benefited from the generosity of many of my clients who have submitted to in-depth interviews on the subject of influence. Most would only speak on condition of anonymity – indicating a self-consciousness, no doubt, about acknowledging their own influential status and a wariness of disclosing their modus operandi – but they are mostly quoted verbatim here on the way influence is acquired, honed and best deployed.

Along the way, my research has largely dispelled four pervasive myths about influence.

The first myth is that it is a skill, like public speaking or playing the flute. Equip people with a set of techniques, proponents of this approach suggest, and they can be applied in any situation. Influence is a process that can be done 'to' someone. Give me half an hour in the boss's office and I'll 'influence' him round to my way of thinking – it's a sort of layman's hypnosis. This is complete nonsense. If I did indeed manage to influence my boss in that half-hour conversation, the result is much more likely to have been achieved because of the credibility I have built up in his eyes over a long period than any verbal sorcery that came out of my mouth on the spur of the moment. The acquisition of influence is a long-term process. It is the gradual accumulation of credibility over time, and it is a strategy far more than a skill.

The second myth is that anyone who aspires to be influential must be a modern-day Machiavelli, a creature of the night, dark, devious and willing to stop at nothing to achieve his dastardly aims. A range of lurid and occasionally bestselling non-fiction titles has contributed to this caricature. The truth is rather more mundane. Yes, a streak of ruthlessness is sometimes required to consolidate a position of influence. There is certainly a need to keep your friends close and your enemies closer. But influence is more effectively achieved by nobler attributes: a fertile imagination, a keen work ethic, a talent for getting on with people. Keen students of the 'dark arts' of political intrigue are likely to be disappointed with most (but not all) of what follows.

Another, and possibly more pervasive, myth is that influence is the inevitable reward for a lifetime of hard work and honest endeavour. Put in the hours, this theory runs, keep your nose clean, establish a track record of modest achievement and you will become influential by default. This is wishful thinking. Most of the people I talked to fell into one of two distinct categories. They either excelled at something – they were subject-matter experts or highly skilled practitioners – or they were extremely skilful at orchestrating people and events to enable them to achieve their objectives. There was mostly a plan or a talent at work; it was rarely about simply serving time.

Finally, despite what our celebrity-obsessed culture may suggest, you don't need to be famous to be influential. None of the people interviewed for this book is in the public eye, yet all have been able to achieve what they wanted in organizations large and small.

Before I give an overview of the factors that *are* relevant in becoming influential, it is worth exploring briefly the context in which influence is acquired today. Until fairly recently, influence could be secured only with the involvement and co-operation of other people. A novelist needed a publisher; a journalist needed a supportive editor. Politicians obviously relied on the machinery of their parties, and businesspeople on the approval of their directors and their shareholders. Having an idea or a talent was not enough – you needed the assistance of others to reach an audience. The social skills were therefore as important as the creative ones – getting people onside, working effectively in a team, playing the system, abiding by the rules mattered as much as the quality of the thought or innovation.

The Internet changed all that. Now it is possible to acquire influence without a support system. It's not just the President of the United States or the CEO of General Electric who gets to shape opinion – it's a lone blogger in New Jersey who catches a wave. 'Ideas that spread win,' says Seth Godin, a social commentator who himself personifies this new brand of influence. To be influential in this space, it is all about the quality, the freshness and the creativity of the idea. So, if your aim is to gain influence using a laptop and a broadband connection, there are a few basic principles that might help you in Part 1 of this book.

For the rest of us, working away in organizations large and small, it's not just the purity of the thought that counts: it's the way we play the system. The other parts of the book are intended to help you with that.

So just how do we become influential? It seems to be a combination of five factors: what you think; who you know; what you do; who you are – and how you play the game. This book groups the 50 influencing strategies under these five headings. In which areas do you see yourself exerting influence?

1 What you think

If this is the age of ideas, you come up with more than your fair share. This is the route to influence for the innovators, the creatives and the mould-breakers. You think differently.

You express your fresh thinking powerfully. And there is a great opportunity here for 'solopreneurs', people who don't necessarily need an organization to achieve influence – just brilliant, imaginative thinking and access to an audience. *Exemplar:* Malcolm Gladwell

2 Who you know

Other people are the means of your ascent, and I don't mean that disparagingly. You are extremely skilled at making alliances, bringing people together and getting the best out of others. You see a team as greater than the sum of its parts. *Exemplar:* Alex Ferguson

3 What you do

You have honed your own productivity until it is the envy of the competition. You personally produce more or better than other people. Your influence stems largely from an unarguable track record of achievement. *Exemplar:* Roger Federer

4 Who you are

You make an impression on everyone you meet. You are supremely aware of your strengths and confident in your abilities. You make a strong personal impact and are the sort of person others feel compelled to follow. You will also evade easy categorization – perhaps you could be proficient across several fields. *Exemplar:* Steve Jobs

5 How well you play the game

You have a true politician's appreciation of the delicate balance of power and are able to build support for your own agenda and marginalize opponents. You are adept at using the levers of power and can be ruthless in your pursuit of it. *Exemplar:* Lyndon B. Johnson

These, then, are the five key areas the book will consider. The genuinely influential appear to excel in more than one of these areas, but don't feel you need to master them all! You will notice that some of the ideas seem contradictory – in defence of which I can only say that there is more than one way to skin a cat. These strategies are for dipping into and experimenting with: I hope you find some practical and actionable help here, and that these techniques help you achieve more of what you feel you deserve.

This SECRETS book contains a number of special textual features, which have been developed to help you navigate the chapters quickly and easily. Throughout the book, you will find these indicated by the following icons:

Each chapter contains **quotes** from inspiring figures. These will be useful for helping you understand different viewpoints and why each secret is useful in a practical context.

Also included in each chapter are three **strategies** that outline techniques for putting this secret into practice.

The **putting it all together** box at the end of each chapter provides a summary of each chapter, and a quick way into the core concepts of each secret.

Part 1

What you know: influence through ideas

I Simplify

John Turner, a junior partner at a global accountancy practice, felt uneasy as he settled into the back of a cab in the darkness of a February morning. It wasn't the early start that had disturbed him – he was used to those. No, it was his destination – the studios of Bloomberg Television – where he was to participate in a live breakfast-time interview on the effect of the credit crunch on small and medium-sized British businesses.

He had never been on television before. He had only had a half-day of media training a couple of years previously. He was relatively junior. He felt like a fraud. He reached for his phone and gave his head of department a call. Mike Collins, one of the firm's most senior partners, answered the call straight away.

'Mike, I'm on my way to this Bloomberg thing and I'm panicking a bit. Are you sure I'm the best qualified to do it? Shouldn't this be your territory, or someone else with a bit more gravitas than me?'

Collins's reply was unequivocal.

'It's breakfast time, John. Gravitas is the last thing people want – it will send them back to sleep. Do what you do in team meetings – tell it like it is. Demystify all the BS. You'll be fine.'

Emboldened, 45 minutes later John found himself under the bright lights of the studio floor, sitting across the table from Bloomberg's breakfast-time anchor.

'So, John Turner, perhaps you can help us understand the implications of the latest economic data…'

He picked up the baton without pausing.

'Francine, there's a lot of hot air around at the moment on this subject but when you get down to it, what British business is most concerned about are the 3 Ls: leverage, liquidity and liability. So let's see how this new data impacts on each of these…'

Later in the day, John bumped into Mike Collins.

'Great job this morning, John. Really good response from our clients.'

'Hope I did OK…'

'You did fantastic. It's a real gift you've got. I could have thrown 20 more senior people at that interview and I guarantee they would have done a great job of making a complex situation even more complex. You stripped it down to its bare essentials, which is why everyone wants you on the end of a phone…'

AIM FOR SIMPLICITY + MEMORABILITY

I lose count of the number of people I come across who have achieved positions of influence because of their communication style. And the winning style shows remarkable consistency: simplicity is its hallmark. Being able to boil an argument down to its bare essentials and convey the essence of a concept in plain language – this is a highly valued trait.

Less is always more: fewer sentences; fewer syllables; and fewer slides. This is usually the result of hard work; great communicators tend to be ruthless editors of their own material, which is refined and refined until the greatest effect is achieved with the fewest words.

One of my interviewees put it this way:

'I have noticed how highly prized clarity is. You can have the best idea in the world but, unless you can communicate it clearly in the first 30 seconds, people start switching off. So before big meetings I will always take a few moments to gather my thoughts and consider the **three key points** I want to make. I will sometimes boil it down to just three key words – I ask myself: 'What three key words do I want people to remember about this proposal or idea'?'

Closely aligned with simplicity is memorability and if you can combine the two you have a winning formula. John Turner in our earlier example used **alliteration** to good effect. Rather than his three key words being random, he had them all begin with the same letter. Cheesy? Possibly. Memorable? You bet.

Likewise, the occasional **rhyme** can boost your memorability. Sin Bin. Brain Drain. Analysis Paralysis. These are all phrases I expect you have heard. They are all concepts that have stood the test of time. They are not necessarily the most astute or brilliant of insights, but the packaging was simplicity + memorability: a short phrase coupled with a rhyme.

MAKE LESS NOISE; INCREASE THE SIGNAL

Give people an opportunity not to engage with your message and they will probably take it. An important aspect of getting your ideas taken seriously is to ensure the minimum level of distraction – and people are often their own worst enemies in this regard.

Things that frequently get in the way of the message we want to send are unconscious repetition, vagueness and the pointless use of acronyms and abbreviations. Distracting body language such as shuffling papers or twiddling pens is another common way of diverting your audience's attention away from your key points.

We have all sat through meetings and presentations where we have put up with people poring anxiously over their notes or wasting time with endless context-setting and 'background' information without ever getting to the point.

I'm sure that you can add your own pet peeve to the list.

The point is that all of this activity dilutes the message. It is extraneous.

When you have formulated your idea or proposal in such a way that it can be delivered with simplicity, don't undermine it with your own distracting mannerisms. Get out of the way, and get to the point.

GO UNPLUGGED

Another threat to simplicity in communication is our reliance on technology. How many presentations have you attended where because of an 'IT' failing, the whole event sank like a stone?

Sure, multimedia presentations can be compelling when done well. Images, data and statistics can look great flashed up on the big screen. But there is always the risk of technological meltdown. And often we will need to do our influencing not in a plush lecture theatre where a captive audience hangs on our every word, but over an imperfect telephone line being interrupted by five other speakers.

Don't assume that technology will conceal your own inadequacy. Instead, make sure that you can make your point without the need for fancy diagrams or animations. Steve Jobs, who is often viewed as the exemplar of this kind of communication, ironically enough didn't rely on technology for his presentational power. He used slides but they usually contained just one simple phrase or a single high-quality image. The real impact was made by the man himself, in black, pacing the stage without notes, giving his real-time demonstrations of whatever technology he was launching. One man and a prop captured the attention of the world.

The way we prepare to communicate our ideas is often the root of confused or confusing thinking. We will often reach first for the computer or the notepad and start to draft our ideas as if putting together an essay or a treatise. Crucially, though, our ideas need to be heard rather than read, and that requires a different kind of composition.

Work it all out in your head *before* writing it down. Usually, when I make this suggestion in workshops, people are aghast. 'I've got so much to say,' they will remark. 'How can I possibly remember it all?' And that is exactly the point. If you can't remember it without recourse to voluminous notes or spreadsheets, what hope does your audience have of understanding the import of what you wanted to say?

Putting it all together

If your idea or point of view resists simplification – if it cannot be expressed in language a child would understand – there's probably something wrong with it. Maybe you have seen the tortuous pitches people sometimes give on the TV show *Dragon's Den*? They stand in the spotlight in front of potential investors, their big moment has arrived, and they are incapable of articulating exactly what their product or service is, let alone how it would benefit from investment.

The ability to simplify – to make the complex accessible – is a key skill of the influential.

- What are the three key words that encapsulate your idea/proposal/contribution to a meeting?
- What distracting mannerisms do you need to control?
- Can you reduce your reliance on technology to influence and persuade?

2 Identify

> ❝ 'As a designer, you've always got to push yourself forward; you've always got to keep up with the trends or make your own trends. That's what I do.' **Alexander McQueen**

> ❝ 'You have to stay updated on trends, social things and pop culture, you need to stay with the times and keep evolving.' **Corey Feldman**

> ❝ 'I don't set trends. I just find out what they are and exploit them.' **Dick Clark**

> ❝ 'I like inventing stories. Very often it's exciting to write about an imaginary future based on trends, you work out what things could wind up as.' **Nigel Kneale**

> ❝ 'It's hard to go with a trend. As soon as it's out, everyone picks it up. It's important to stay true to yourself. Have fun with fashion instead of letting it dictate.' **Estella Warren**

Tipping points. Black swans. Generation X. These phrases have achieved the influencer's holy grail: they have entered the language, have outlined their initial context and are used in their own right over and over again every day around the world.

Malcolm Gladwell, Nasim Nicholas Taleb and Douglas Coupland – the originators, respectively, of these three phrases – are perfect exponents of this influencing tactic. Not only did they identify three trends or phenomena: the moment at which a (metaphorical) trickle becomes a flood; major unexpected events that are sometimes wrongly rationalized after the event; and the fact that a generation of people can share certain attitudes and traits. They also came up with a memorable phrase to encapsulate the trend and sear it on the listener's brain.

Your objective need not be to become part of the global vernacular (though why not?). The ability to notice a trend and apply a vivid label to it can turn you into a poet or a philosopher in your own organization, arena or even household! None of the three examples uses advanced verbal pyrotechnics – you don't have to be a lyricist in the Bob Dylan mould to use this technique. It's about simple, colourful phrases attached to concepts visible to anyone but packaged brilliantly by you.

We so often default to the bland in our everyday communication. From the deadness of the email subject line – 'Tomorrow's Meeting', 'Catch-up Call' – to the banal predictability of so many PowerPoint presentations – 'Budget Forecast Update Q1' – the bar for being memorable is set reassuringly low. Any attempt you make to liven up a presentation or meeting through the language you use is likely to win you some credit.

A knack for delivering the memorable phrase is undoubtedly a common trait of the genuinely influential. From Churchill's Iron Curtain to Mandela's Rainbow Nation, the best leaders have known the power of a simple phrase. These politicians were often able to rely on an army of professional speechwriters, of course, but if you follow the principles that follow, you should be able to come up with a few purple pearls of your own…

SAY IT IN METAPHOR

Sun Tzu wrote the *Art of War* in about 500 BCE, but it remains a favourite text for leaders everywhere. Its popularity is surely due in part to our thirst for metaphor and analogy: not many of the Chinese general's twenty-first-century readers will be tasked with turning 180 concubines into soldiers as Sun Tzu apparently was, but there is something inherently pleasing about comparing the rules of ancient warfare with the challenges of our own lives, businesses and careers.

If you can take a concept from a popular but unrelated field – television, for example, or a sport, or a phenomenon from the natural world – and apply it to a trend you want to talk about, you can often imprint your thinking indelibly on other people's brains.

I show two slides in a talk I give about building a network: one is a picture of a frog; the other a picture of a bat. I'm making a simple point: some people are reactive and laze around in their ponds all day waiting for a juicy fly to drop in on them. Others are more proactive, make a point of getting out, covering the territory and seeking out their prey. Which are you, I ask the audience: frog or bat?

It's not a particularly apposite analogy, but it never fails to generate a buzz of excited chatter in the room. And once, years after my session, I saw one of the delegates again. 'I remember you,' she said. 'You're the frog and bat man!'

Next time you want to make a point or an observation, particularly to a large audience, why not consider expressing yourself metaphorically? Maybe your organization used to share the properties of a lion, but now it needs to become more of a cheetah: greater win ratios but smaller prey. Or perhaps your team has become so concerned with defending its territory that it has stopped thinking about the need to score a few goals of its own? Perhaps the cultural shift you are trying to achieve is akin to a PC user encountering his first Mac?

The more vivid your word picture, the more easily your audience can relate to the original idea; and the chances of your idea gaining traction and spreading are increased exponentially.

THINK IN FOUR BOXES

While you have been reading this chapter, someone, somewhere has drawn the growth/share matrix on a whiteboard somewhere and asked a class of students to consider the implications of too many question marks versus too few cash cows and all the other permutations that arise from the most celebrated four-box model of all time.

Developed by the Boston Consulting Group way back in 1970, the matrix uses two sets of variables (rate of growth and market share) and applies labels to the four combinations to provide an accessible framework for discussing, in this case, an organization's product portfolio. And if longevity is the ultimate proof of influence, this framework (aka the Boston Box) must be in the premier league as it closes in on its 50th birthday.

Four-box models have for years made money for business consultants everywhere and can come in handy for you, too. If anything has two clear sets of parameters – time and money, say, or size and speed – get drawing your two axes, put a label on your four boxes, and start being seen as some sort of pedagogical Picasso.

Sometimes, a critical role in meetings is giving shape or structure to the discussion, and authoring a four-box model can help do that. It's money for old rope – but don't tell the business consultants I told you.

USE THE RULE OF THREE

Another way of communicating an insight in such a way that it stands a chance of being retained and perhaps achieving a life of its own is to divide it into its constituent parts. And there is no doubt that three is the magic number in this context.

All the way from Julius Caesar, who came, saw and conquered, to Tony Blair whose three priorities were education, education and education – via the American constitutionalists' appeal to life, liberty and the pursuit of happiness – three has had almost mystical rhetorical properties. Maybe it's because we divide existence into past, present and future, so the rule of three is almost hard-wired into us.

When you next present your ideas, eschew the 16 bullet points in favour of a snappy rule of three. Things get understood in threes. Things get remembered in threes. Working with this principle – 'I think there are three phases we need to work through…' 'There are probably three acts to this drama – recognition, redirection and renewal. And we're not even at recognition phase yet…' – can transform your impact (especially when combined with a little alliteration, as in the last example).

Again, this doesn't have to be clever. It simply combines two fundamentals of influential communication: simplicity and memorability.

Putting it all together

Some of this may sound outside your comfort zone: if you like to think of yourself as a plain speaker, this stuff may seem just a bit too contrived or, well, cheesy to get your buy-in. Think again. One of the surest ways to influence is to stand out from the crowd, and because so much of business life is conducted in a bland monochrome, some modest creativity of thought can provoke a surprisingly positive response. It is not the individuals with the greatest insight who gain the most influence, but those who can communicate their insight with impact and clarity.

- What are the key trends or developments in your field or industry that people have yet to pay much attention to?
- What opportunities do you have to draw these trends to other people's attention?
- Can you use the tricks of the scriptwriter's trade – metaphor, analogy, four-box model or rule of three – to communicate your insight in a bright, original way?

3 Entice

> 'A good teacher, like a good entertainer, first must hold his audience's attention, then he can teach his lesson.'
> John Henrik Clarke

> 'I did know that the book would end with a mind-boggling trial, but I didn't know exactly how it would turn out. I like a little suspense when I am writing, too.' James Patterson

> 'I conclude ... NOTHING. The conclusions ... EMERGE. I'm not the one who reaches a conclusion. You (audience member) reach the conclusion via the stories I've told and the data I'll present... I am shoving nothing down your throat. You are doing the work. You are figuring it out.' Tom Peters

> 'A poem with grandly conceived and executed stanzas, such as one of Keats's odes, should be like an enfilade of rooms in a palace: one proceeds, with eager anticipation, from room to room.' James Fenton

> 'A man is only a leader when a follower stands beside him.'
> Mark Brouwer

Without an audience, you have no influence. Whether it's a real-life audience that sits in front of you for your presentation, or a virtual one that tunes in regularly to hear your podcast or read your blog, you need to cultivate an audience.

The question is, with so much competition, how are you going to reach it? The temptation is to try and shout louder, to yell to be heard above the din of everyday life, but this is not always the best way of getting noticed.

We own two cats, and, as you will know if you have cats yourself, they are fairly independent creatures. One day, one of them decided to take a walk on the wild side. He climbed up one of the outside walls of the house, and once he'd reached the top he stood on a narrow parapet, peering down at our startled faces 10 metres below. Fearful that he might fall, my instinct was to bellow at him. 'George! Get down! Get down this minute!' The louder I roared, the more nonchalantly he averted his gaze. So I got the ladder out and clambered up the steps until he was nearly within clutching distance. Every time I tried to reach for him he moved further away. We ended up staring at each other across the rooftop as my ladder began to creak...

Then my wife had an idea. She simply filled a saucer with milk and left it on the doorstep far below. As soon as the china hit the paving stone, George's ears pricked up and he set off down the nearest drainpipe like a thunderbolt. Happily lapping his milk, he kept one eye firmly fixed on me as I gingerly tottered down the stepladder to join him on terra firma.

The point, as I am sure you realize, is that enticement is sometimes more effective than predation. Ideally, we want to draw our audience towards us of their own free will rather than giving chase and dragging them back to our cave kicking and screaming.

So what is your equivalent of the saucer of milk? What can you put forward that is seductive and enticing and draws people willingly into your orbit?

OFFER AN INDUCEMENT (A LEGAL ONE!)

We don't have to go too far from the saucer of milk principle to draw in a human, as opposed to a feline, audience.

Food and drink may be old school, but it works. I run a lot of lunchtime events, and the ones where the free sandwiches are laid on are always the best attended. I am totally cool with this, and so should you be. Until you are uber-influential, in the Seth Godin/Malcolm Gladwell category, your name alone is not going to draw a crowd. I don't care what inducement is offered to get bums on seats – I just want an audience. And my hope is that, having come along for the sandwiches, they are pleasantly surprised by the content of my talk and may come back again.

Other inducements – aside from a pile of used notes in a brown paper bag – include professional or personal development. People in some professions, such as law and accounting, actually need to show that they have put time into professional development in order to keep practising. Help them tick that box while at the same time knocking their socks off and giving them an opportunity to network.

For an online forum, it's likely to be a mix of personal development and convenience. Give them enough takeaways (as in the 'how-to' post in Chapter 8) in as short a time as possible and, providing you are assisting with a pretty basic human need (make money, save time, lose weight, stay happy), the audience should build.

PRACTISE THE ART OF SUSPENSE

Understandably, we are keen to offer great value to our audiences, and to that end we sometimes confuse quantity with quality. We stuff our presentations full of detail, and provide reams of appendices as well, just in case any questions were left unanswered. We bombard clients with e-alerts multiple times every month, regardless of need or relevance.

Dickens has a lesson for us here. It is sometimes forgotten that his novels were not released complete to his Victorian audience. Instead, they were serialized – monthly or, occasionally, weekly. This drip, drip effect had the great benefit of building up anticipation. The next instalment was awaited eagerly: it became an event.

The lesson for us in building an audience is to hold a little back. Instead of taking an hour-and-a-half of someone's time all in one go, take 40 minutes three times over. Instead of giving all the answers, let the audience work out some for themselves. Make it puzzling and fun.[1]

---

1 Did anyone notice the deliberate mistake in this paragraph, for example?

Some of the most influential presenters I have seen recently are quite comfortable with sowing a little mystery in their audience – and, by doing so, they become more compelling than those who follow the standard advice and 'tell you what they're going to say, say it, then tell you what they said'.

Why not set the audience a puzzle, or ask a difficult question at the start and then promise you will tell them the answer at the end of the talk? Better still, set a problem at the end of your podcast and promise the answer when the audience joins you for the next episode.

Sometimes, influence comes not from the density of your content but from the breathing spaces you allow within it.

SLIPSTREAM AND PIGGYBACK

Any commercial property expert will tell you that footfall in a shopping mall comes down to one key factor: having an attractive 'anchor' tenant. This is usually a big-name department store such as John Lewis or M&S in the UK and Macy's or Nordstrom in the United States, with the capacity to attract hordes of paying punters. The theory is that, once done with the behemoth, shoppers will wander down the mall and call into the little shoe shop, the delicatessen and the bespoke hi-fi store. It is an enticement strategy akin to slipstreaming: slip in behind the big boys and you have the chance of a free ride.

This has relevance as you try to build your audience; if you can attract a speaker or an interviewee with a bigger profile than yours, you can piggyback on their audience and perhaps convert a few into your own.

But why would a successful figure headline your show just so that you get some exposure? It may be out of generosity, a sense of 'giving something back'; or maybe your project is something they feel strongly about on a values level; or maybe it is just good old-fashioned ego – they find it hard to turn down the opportunity to appear on a podcast entitled, say, 'Secrets of Influential People'.

Brad is a blogger who built an audience by interviewing popular bloggers:

'It seemed like a no-brainer. I got to speak to some great people, who were more often than not willing to dish out their insights on how to build an audience, while at the same time acquiring a slice of their, not inconsiderable, audiences! The secret is to keep their time commitment short, treat them with the utmost professionalism and, if they say no, not bug them.'

Putting it all together

The road to ruin has been the result for many who have followed the delusional maxim 'Build it and they will come'. Make no mistake: if you seek to build influence from the ground up on the back of your ideas or your imagination, you will need to hustle to build an audience. Use every trick in this (and any other) book to ensure that there are people devouring your content and – all being well – sharing it.

- What can you offer an audience as an inducement to engage with you, over and above your brilliant content and effortless charm?
- How can you build up some curiosity, some suspense?
- Who can you contact who would be a big box-office draw? What would be in it for them if they were to help you out?

4 Contrast

66 *'We stand today on the edge of a new frontier – the frontier of the 1960s – a frontier of unknown opportunities and perils – a frontier of unfulfilled hopes and threats.'* John F. Kennedy

66 *'Writing has laws of perspective, of light and shade just as painting does, or music. If you are born knowing them, fine. If not, learn them. Then rearrange the rules to suit yourself.'*
Truman Capote

66 *'You couldn't have strength without weakness, you couldn't have light without dark, you couldn't have love without loss.'*
Jodi Picoult

66 *'There are as many nights as days, and the one is just as long as the other in the year's course. Even a happy life cannot be without a measure of darkness, and the word "happy" would lose its meaning if it were not balanced by sadness.'* C.G. Jung

66 *'Study the past, if you would divine the future.'* Confucius

The purpose of influence is to change something. Whether you are trying to influence colleagues in a meeting or Internet surfers on the other side of the world, your starting premise is that you want them to stop doing that and start doing this. The 'this' could be a new way of thinking or behaving or purchasing or living, but it definitely requires a modification of 'that'.

In order to change *that* into *this*, a journey needs to take place – but people are unlikely to set out on a journey until the destination has been made clear to them. They need to understand that this new destination offers some benefit over the status quo. And the way great influencers have done that over the years is to be adept at the simple rhetorical skill of contrast: they consciously draw a distinction between *here* and *there*.

Two of the most influential speeches of the twentieth century were based on a finely wrought contrast. Martin Luther King, in his speech at the Lincoln Memorial in 1963, contrasted the reality of life for the black person – who 'still languished in the corners of American society and finds himself an exile in his own land' – with the hope of a better future where 'my four little children will one day live in a nation where they will not be judged by the colour of their skin but by the content of their character'.

Two years earlier, newly elected President John F. Kennedy contrasted the origin of the 'same solemn oath our forebears prescribed nearly a century and three-quarters ago' with the new generation of Americans 'born in this century, tempered by war, disciplined by a hard and bitter peace, proud of our ancient heritage', who were now taking command. And then came one of the most famous contrast-based rhetorical flourishes of them all: 'And so, my fellow Americans: ask not what your country can do for you – ask what you can do for your country.'

Generally, change – as anyone who has tried to commit to a new year's resolution will know – is pretty tough. By using this device, you can clearly articulate the benefit of the effort, and you will stand a chance of motivating people to act in the way you advocate.

USE SIMPLE CHRONOLOGY

The two celebrated examples above use chronology for their contrast. They make it clear that the past is not the present, and that the future must look different from today.

A team manager might make a point of reviewing progress in the last quarter to ensure that due credit is given, but would then always look ahead to the next quarter and set challenging targets. Past performance, as every fund manager knows, is not necessarily a guide to future achievement, but in this case a poor quarter would instil a determination to do better next time; a good quarter, publicly recognized, would often spur people on to even greater things.

The point is that to persuade you need a frame of reference. If you want to lead us to a better future, we need to be made aware of just how bad it is today. Juxtaposing the *detail* of present reality with the *outline* of an aspirational future is a technique politicians have been using to influence voters for generations. Without the relentless focus on the job losses, the increase in the cost of living and the non-existent pay rise, the utopia of a better tomorrow would look far less attractive. You can use the same technique.

Be unflinching in your assessment of the deficiencies and disappointments you want to change because that will give you leverage in motivating people to change course.

USE PEER-GROUP COMPARISON

We know that social proof is an extremely strong motivator in getting people to do things. We look at the reviews on Amazon and, if there seem to be plenty of five-star responses, we are more comfortable making our purchase. The same is true at an organizational level: most sectors have their league tables or award ceremonies where they get to assess the strength of the competition. This can be a way of persuading and influencing, as Kieron, a CMO at a pharmaceutical organization, relates:

'Whenever I need to influence the board, there's one piece of data I know I need to have in place beforehand, and that's what our competitors are doing. If I can contrast our approach with that of the competition, particularly the boys who are slightly bigger than us, it always gets me a hearing. It doesn't necessarily mean that they agree, but they will certainly listen. People will say that they want to do things their way, that they have a unique model and so on. But if you can say that we're out of step with the rest of the market here, people will listen.'

There is a big opportunity here for consultancy businesses, too. With large businesses being by and large concerned with their own operations and internal politics, the consultant who can give a broader view of the market, and in particular a sense of what the competition is up to, has a real chance to influence.

DEPICT THE THREATS – AND THEN THE OPPORTUNITIES

We discuss the concept of loss aversion elsewhere in this book. Suffice it to say that people are more motivated to keep what they already have than to go out and seize what they don't. This is why inertia is such a strong factor in many teams: if things are reasonably OK, why change them?

As an influencer, you will need to articulate precisely why the status quo is not sustainable, and you can do that by outlining the nature of the threats that face your business, your team or your line of work. Real threats challenge inertia because they make it clear that, if we do nothing, we stand to lose.

The step that prevents you from sounding like a scaremonger or a corporate Cassandra is contrast. Depict the threats in all their gruesome glory, sure. But also see the opportunities within those threats. Take your audience from darkness to the promise of light.

'The bad stuff always gets people's attention,' continues Kieron. 'Government X has announced that it will reduce healthcare spending in the next fiscal year by 3 per cent in real terms. (Bad news for us.) But it actually has no idea about how to achieve that. If we partner with them, examining ways in which they can make some savings, our longer-term dominance in this market may be assured. (Good news.)'

Any designer worth his or her salt will use contrast all the time as one of the key aesthetic principles of their work. This includes contrast in colour, contrast in shape and size, and contrast in direction.

What works so well in the visual arts is also very powerful in argument, debate and presentation. We need to be as aware of what we are arguing *against* as what we are arguing *for*, and to be able to draw effective contrast between both.

You need to provide a frame of reference for the debate. A visitor from outer space would only be able to guess the size of an orange if you presented a golf ball and a watermelon and said it lay somewhere between the two. Likewise, the size of the opportunity you want to people to visualize may only be apparent through the judicious use of comparison and contrast.

- How can the past be used to highlight changes required in the future?
- What stories or data can you put forward about your competitors that compel colleagues to act?
- What are the threats that challenge the status quo?

5 Dissent

> 'If a man does not keep pace with his companions, perhaps it is because he hears a different drummer. Let him step to the music which he hears, however measured or far away.'
> Henry David Thoreau

> 'I try to deny myself any illusions or delusions, and I think that this perhaps entitles me to try and deny the same to others, at least as long as they refuse to keep their fantasies to themselves.' Christopher Hitchens

> 'To a contrarian like me, constant advice not to do something almost always starts me quickly down the risky, unpopular path.' Michael Bloomberg

> 'You have enemies? Good. That means you've stood up for something, some time in your life.' Winston Churchill

> 'Be daring, be different, be impractical, be anything that will assert integrity of purpose and imaginative vision against the play-it-safers, the creatures of the commonplace, the slaves of the ordinary.' Cecil Beaton

Although we humans are social animals, we do still have a fundamental choice: to be part of the crowd or to stand out from it. In the hurly-burly of everyday life, however, we rarely recognize this as a real choice. Social norms are so powerful, the advertising and promotion industries so sophisticated, and groupthink so prevalent, that more often than not we get swept

23

along with the crowd. Whether we are choosing a book at a bookshop or giving weary assent to some proposal at a meeting, we tend to 'go with the flow' and do what the majority seems to favour, since this seems to represent the lowest-risk option.

Throughout history, however, there has been a small but influential band of individuals who have chosen a different path. Where there is a trend, they buck it. Where there are rules, they bend them. Where there is apparent consensus, they dissent. From Galileo to Winston Churchill to Rosa Parks, the willingness to be contrarian, to offer an unfashionable – even heretical – opposing view, has brought certain individuals more than their fair share of attention (in some cases, not all of it welcome). And by offering a dissenting view, they have become opinion formers rather than opinion followers.

You need a thick skin to be a contrarian. Those who dare to challenge the status quo are rarely welcomed with open arms – you can expect plenty of short-term unpopularity. You also need fine judgement: those who oppose too often, who gain a reputation as naysayers or prophets of doom, are likely to be dismissed as irrelevant Cassandras.

Nevertheless, there are plenty of opportunities in daily life to offer a contrarian view in a way that will help boost your profile and make you stand out, if only for a moment or so, from the crowd. It requires a combination of bravery and tact; but because it is so unusual, it offers unique rewards for those willing to give it a go.

DON'T FOLLOW FASHION

Warren Buffet is one of the richest men in the world. His fortune currently stands in excess of $50 billion. Inevitably, a cottage industry has sprung up around trying to divine the secrets of his success, to communicate his investment wisdom to the masses. In fact, the man himself expresses the key to his investment strategy pretty succinctly: 'We simply attempt to be fearful when others are greedy and to be greedy only when others are fearful.' That's a contrarian approach in a nutshell. When the rest of the investment world was drawn towards ever more complex financial instruments in ever more unlikely markets, Buffet was resolutely unfashionable. He continued to invest in the unloved, the unpopular and the undervalued. And he continued to build a fortune while investors in derivatives – he memorably referred to these as 'financial weapons of mass destruction' – were burned.

The allure of the new can be overwhelming. We make decisions based on what seems to be 'cutting edge' or the 'next big thing'. Sometimes, it pays to offer a less sexy but better-balanced view.

The next time you hear the unmistakeable sound of a bandwagon gathering speed, why not ask everyone to pause and reflect? There are probably other options worth considering – safer, less alluring ones. It may be that you can't stop the bandwagon, but at least if it crashes you'll be the one to emerge with your reputation enhanced rather than in tatters.

STAND UP AND BE COUNTED

Have you ever been in a meeting or a conversation where you've begun to get the sneaking feeling that everyone else is completely and utterly mad? You have had a sense that they were either missing the obvious or focusing too much on the irrelevant, or that they were utterly unaware of their assumptions and biases.

If so, you'll probably have kept quiet, waited for the uneasy feeling to pass, and left the conversation wondering why on earth you didn't have the guts to speak up.

Such occasions present a risk-and-reward situation. The risk in offering a contrarian view that turns out to be wrong is probably a bit of a short-term embarrassment. On the other hand, the potential reward of offering a view that is subsequently proved right can be transformative.

Nouriel Roubini was in just this position. As a middle-ranking economist who had done stints at the IMF and the World Bank, he had had a solid but unspectacular career. But then he realized, in the summer of 2006, that his view of the global economy was diverging radically from the consensus of his peers. Should he keep quiet and agree with the majority that boom times were here to stay? Or should he speak out, express a different view and invite the ridicule of others?

He spoke out. He gave a speech to the IMF warning of a 'once-in-a-lifetime housing bust' followed by 'the global financial system shuddering to a halt'. It was certainly contrarian at the time and found favour with very few economists or commentators. But Roubini also happened to be right. These days, he is hailed as a prophet and is one of the highest-profile economists in the world.

So the next time you get that sneaking feeling…

BE PERSISTENT

We have established that the contrarian view is unlikely to win much support in the short term. A judgement call is then needed: how long do you continue to voice a 'left-field' view? The answer is: not for ever, but probably for longer than you think.

Successful entrepreneurs get used to this cycle of rejection after rejection followed by eventual acclaim. Clarence Birdseye, the founder of the frozen-food industry, went bankrupt in 1924 because of a lack of public interest in this new-fangled method of preserving food. He went back to his factory, perfected his system, and sold the patent in 1929 for $22 million, roughly equivalent to $250 million in today's money.

Not all of us are blessed with this sort of resilience. It is easy, though, to fall into the trap of imagining other people have all the answers. Entrepreneurs, by contrast, seem to have got failure in proportion. Instead of being paralysed by it, they look at pragmatically: if I crash and burn this time, I must be that much nearer to success the next.

The prospect of being a lone voice may not appeal – you will feel exposed, certainly, and may come under attack. But you will also earn the respect of those who know that they'd never have the guts to put themselves in the firing line. And if you happen to express a view that goes on to become widely accepted as truth, the implications for your career or life could be considerable.

No one likes a whinger, just as no one likes someone trying to score points or seem cleverer than other people. Tone is critical for a contrarian. Have the courage to express your view, but do it with a certain amount of humility. The best contrarians are those who don't force their view down other people's throats, but offer up a stimulating alternative for discussion.

- When did you last offer a contrarian view?
- How quickly do you drop an opinion if it doesn't get immediate support?
- How often do you submit to a consensus view simply because you don't have the energy to make your own case?

6 Borrow

> 'If I have seen further, it is by standing on the shoulders of Giants.' Isaac Newton

> 'Those who do not want to imitate anything, produce nothing.' Salvador Dalí

> 'Immature poets imitate; mature poets steal.' T. S. Eliot

> 'Nothing is original. Steal from anywhere that resonates with inspiration or fuels your imagination. Devour old films, new films, music, books, paintings, photographs, poems, dreams, random conversations, architecture, bridges, street signs, trees, clouds, bodies of water, light and shadows. Select only things to steal from that speak directly to your soul. If you do this, your work (and theft) will be authentic. Authenticity is invaluable; originality is non-existent. And don't bother concealing your thievery – celebrate it if you feel like it. In any case, always remember what Jean-Luc Godard said: "It's not where you take things from – it's where you take them to."' Jim Jarmusch

When you dig into their histories, you find that even the most iconic, influential figures of all time were often channelling the work of those who went before. Indeed, it is often their choice of who to copy that gives their work its essential character. Even Shakespeare mined many sources and plundered the work of earlier writers such as Plutarch, Boccaccio and Holinshed for plot, character and narrative arc.

The celebrated neoclassical architecture of, for example, Washington, DC, as seen in the Capitol buildings or the Lincoln Memorial, takes as its inspiration the work of Andrea Palladio, who was active in sixteenth-century Venice, and who himself adapted and reinterpreted the architectural precepts of ancient Rome.

In popular music, the most influential acts of all time, the Beatles and the Rolling Stones, acknowledged their debt to earlier American artists such as Muddy Waters, Chuck Berry and Buddy Holly.

And, in politics, some of the most influential figures of recent times have been keen to invoke the inspirational ghosts of their predecessors, whether it is Thatcher and Churchill or Obama and Lincoln.

Just as an individual's real-life network can boost their influence through association, so too can their historical idols or heroes. The influential, strikingly often, seem to have the humility to recognize greatness, learn from it, and then go on to appropriate some of its clothes for their own. If imitation is the sincerest form of flattery, then many influential people have got the flattery thing down pat.

Who, then, are your heroes? What historical company do you wish to keep? This is not a matter of delusions of grandeur. If you are going to model yourself on anyone, why not take lessons from the very best? In the study of great lives, you may well find inspiration for your own.

QUOTE THE EXPERTS FREELY

There's not a single presentation that can't be enlivened by the judicious use of quotes from the uber-influential. This is not my judgement, but the view of Tom Peters, the grandfather of business gurus and co-author of the seminal book *In Search of Excellence*. Anyone who has seen Tom in action will know that the backdrop to his highly charged, provocative talks is always a parade of quotes written in bold colours and outsize fonts. Anyone from Demosthenes to Bill Gates gets quoted over Tom's shoulder. Here is one of the most fêted business communicators of them all ... and one of his key techniques in his gigs is to quote other people.

To quote the man himself:

'Sure, I add my own views and label them as such. I will not deny it. However, in the main, I will rely on others to carry the day. This is huge. No way to overstate. Speaker-as-medium, not trying to push her or his point of view, but push the Gospel of the Superstars the speaker has invited to join her or him on stage. It's a trick. It's the truth. It works.'

It takes a special kind of insight to appreciate that, however idiosyncratic one's point of view, there's always someone else who said it better. Use the wisdom of acknowledged experts to provide added credibility to arguments of your own.

DRAW AN ANALOGY

There are times when a suggestion you make will be so out of left-field, so beyond the reference of those you are talking to, that to get buy-in you will need to draw an analogy. The lives of the great and good can be useful for that.

Mark, who along with several colleagues lost his job in the wake of the banking crisis, used just this technique.

'I was trying to persuade my erstwhile colleagues that we should set up a new business together. And everyone was so downbeat – OK, we had just lost well-paid jobs, but there had been a substantial pay-off for everyone and my thinking was "This is not the end." But I couldn't get through to the other guys. So I just started riffing on this theme of "great second acts". Churchill came to mind, obviously, and so did Steve Jobs. When Jobs left Apple the first time, everyone thought he was done with pioneering, but he came back again and came up with the greatest inventions of his career with the iPod and the iPhone and so on. And I was just saying, "Look at history…look at what these people have done…just because we're the wrong side of 40 doesn't mean it's game over." And I could see the penny drop and it was like "I may not be Steve Jobs, but yes… you're right…maybe…"'

No situation is entirely without precedent. History will often be able to give you a useful reference point if you are struggling to get your message across. Military campaigns, sporting feats and great cinematic moments have all been used to inspire and influence.

If don't have a story of your own – use someone else's.

IMITATE THE BEST

I have a friend who is a huge fan of Richard Branson. Whenever he gets into a tight spot, he says to himself: 'What would Branson do in this situation?' Of course, he's never met Branson and he has no idea what the Virgin maestro would actually do in any given situation. But he's read enough about the man's philosophy to hazard a guess and to use Branson as a useful counterpoint to his own first instinct.

Someone else copies the communication style of Sheryl Sandberg, the COO of Facebook and the author of *Lean In*.

'I hadn't seen a woman just on stage talking in a conversational style, popping in anecdotes about dropping off her kids at school and being taken completely seriously. I always used to think you had to ape the male style – lectern, PowerPoint, all that sh** – to communicate effectively in a business context. It was a revelation to me.'

I'm not in any sense suggesting you copy the wardrobe of your favourite business leader or the hairstyle of your favourite actor. But surely it makes sense to follow the example of excellent role models, and if you are not blessed with one in real life, why not examine the approach of exemplars in business, sport or the arts? If it's communication you need to improve, watch videos of the great communicators. If it's handling pressure you struggle with, get some tips from the autobiography of a tennis player or a football manager.

Putting it all together

The magpie technique can be of real benefit to influencers. Why not steal the best secrets of people who have a track record of doing what you want to be able to? Critically, if you are going to steal, make sure that you do so from the very best. And maybe, as Shakespeare managed to do, you will even improve on the original by providing your own embellishments.

- Who are your heroes?
- When can you use analogy? Will the analogy help others to understand, sympathize or feel inspired?
- What behaviour, philosophy or approach can you directly copy from an exemplar or idol?

7 Narrate

There's a trick I teach in my presentation training. I get every student to promise that in their next talk they will use the **Magic Sentence**, and observe the body language of the audience after it is uttered. The Magic Sentence is: 'Let me tell you a real-life story about this...'

In response, about 70 per cent of the audience will lean forward, give more eye contact or in some other way demonstrate through their body language that their curiosity has been aroused. That's the power of story. The abstract becomes specific. The theoretical becomes practical. Attention is piqued as a result.

Storytelling in business became quite fashionable a few years ago, with some seriously unfortunate consequences. There's nothing more embarrassing than seeing a bunch of suited professionals attempting to recast their corporate mission as an Aesop's fable. The point about storytelling in business is not that we need to become immersed in the world of fantasy and fiction, but that we understand the mechanics of how a narrative works. If we then apply that understanding to situations where we need to influence, we will engage audiences more quickly and achieve buy-in more efficiently.

We don't need to over-engineer this. A story in this context does not need to have more plot turns than a Grisham thriller. Nor do we need to have delusions of grandeur, where we imagine a hall full of people hanging on our every word as if we were Charles Dickens reborn. The ability to narrate a story effectively should be, along with literacy and numeracy, a fairly basic component of every professional's skillset, to be used over lunch and around the water cooler as well as in presentations and meetings.

Anthropologists tell us that storytelling is as old as the human race itself. If it worked for people sitting around the campfire in Neanderthal times, it probably has a function in helping you sell your idea to key stakeholders or gain you that promotion. The woolly mammoths may have – mostly – disappeared, but the timeless appeal of the story remains.

PERSONALIZE YOUR STORY

A fundamental mistake inexperienced storytellers make is to distance themselves from the material, to hold it at arm's length. Perhaps they imagine that they are imbuing their material with objectivity. This is the short cut to boredom as far as the audience is concerned. A story needs a narrator, and with that role comes some obligation to self-disclose.

Reveal a bit about yourself when you are making a suggestion or trying to influence. Why does the proposed course of action matter to you? What were the circumstances that forced you to these conclusions? What do you think, what do you feel? This sort of thing comes easier to some personality types than others.

Anya was a junior accountant who had some ideas about how her firm should adapt its recruitment policies to attract a wider range of talent. She was asked to present to the board about it.

'It was something I felt, personally, very strongly about. So I began by outlining my background, that I was the first person in my family to get a professional job or go to university, and that throughout I had found the system stacked against me. I felt uncomfortable being so up front about myself, but people afterwards said it made a real impression on them.'

To make a great connection with an audience, to really up the emotional ante, you have to show a bit of yourself. Don't make the mistake of hiding yourself behind the facts and the figures.

BRING IN THE SPECIFICS

The specific always sounds more authentic than the general. Compare the following approaches in a pitch situation:

'We have clients who come to us sometimes and say that they want to invest overseas but don't know the safest way of doing it...'

'We had a client who, like you, wanted to acquire a medium-sized enterprise in Poland. Their timescale was quite challenging: they came to see us in September and wanted the transaction complete by the end of the year. There were a few specifics about that particular jurisdiction that we had to make them aware of immediately...'

The second, I hope you will agree, sounds more authoritative, as if there is a real track record of experience being drawn upon.

A case study gives you the opportunity to demonstrate your competence rather than merely assert it. But the detail is what counts. Even if confidentiality means that names cannot be mentioned, give some texture to your story. When did it happen? Where did it happen? What was the background of the protagonists, and how did they relate to each other?

It's always the detail that people seem to remember when you recount a recent critical incident. Talking about someone arriving at a meeting and rolling up their shirtsleeves is one example. Another might be the fact that a critical call happened as you were about to board the plane for a family holiday, and had your four children screaming in the background throughout. These are the details that many would regards as frivolous and probably omit, but which actually paint a far more compelling picture than the unadorned facts on their own.

GIVE THEM THE WARTS-AND-ALL VERSION

Without conflict, there is no story. 'Happiness', as the French writer de Montherlant put it, 'writes in white ink on a white page.'

While there is a great temptation to whitewash in case studies, to tell our side of things in a way advantageous to ourselves, if we do so we pay a price. No one wants to listen to a vanilla story, devoid of interest and drama. Achievements seem so much more impressive if we get a sense of disaster narrowly averted along the way.

Leave the bad stuff in – the disagreements, the failures, the disappointments. A case study that shows you overcoming difficulty or challenge is more remarkable than one where everything, apparently, went swimmingly from the start. The greatest teaching stories, for internal use of course, are the ones where plenty went wrong, because those are the ones with important lessons to learn from.

Look at the plot of any Hollywood movie. You will see that it contains a clearly defined 'bad guy' and often takes the form of a quest: challenges put in place by the baddie must be overcome if the prize is to be grasped. When you are using a story to illustrate the credentials of your organization or yourself in a pitch or an interview, you might do well to consider, and clearly articulate, what adversity you had to overcome to win the day and what forces or insecurities were ranged against you.

Putting it all together

There is a myth that certain people are 'natural storytellers'. In fact, storytellers are not necessarily born that way; you can make yourself into a decent one by using the principles just outlined, but mainly by realizing that there are many interactions that take place on a daily basis that cry out to be narrated. Stories are influential because we seem to respond to a narrative arc – not just a collection of facts thrown haphazardly together – where a cast of characters go on a journey encountering a range of threats and challenges on the way. Rather than have your audience make up their own stories, keep control of the process and give yourself a leading role.

- What personal disclosure would be appropriate when you next try and 'sell' an idea?
- What case study could you use to demonstrate yourself or your organization operating effectively? What level of detail can you apply?
- Do you shy away from talking about personal or collective failure? When could an example of recovering from a mistake or potential disaster prove inspiring to others?

8 Teach

> 'True teachers are those who use themselves as bridges over which they invite their students to cross; then, having facilitated their crossing, joyfully collapse, encouraging them to create their own.' Nikos Kazantzakis

> 'I have come to believe that a great teacher is a great artist and that there are as few as there are any other great artists. Teaching might even be the greatest of the arts since the medium is the human mind and spirit.' John Steinbeck

> 'A teacher affects eternity; he can never tell where his influence stops.' Henry Adams

> 'The true measure of your education is not what you know, but how you share what you know with others.' Kent Nerburn

> 'There are two kinds of teachers: the kind that fill you with so much quail shot that you can't move, and the kind that just gives you a little prod behind and you jump to the skies.' Robert Frost

Most business books and self-improvement tomes stress the importance of lifelong learning: they will point out that, when an individual stops learning, he's living on borrowed time. Knowledge is certainly a currency that devalues fairly quickly. What is not so often examined is the other side of the coin: that, in order to learn, we need teachers. And in a world where we are constantly reminded of the pace of change and the way what we thought of as 'cutting edge' can become obsolete overnight, there is a huge opportunity to become influential by being an effective teacher. The thirst for new knowledge, skill and opportunity is a vast, unquenchable market.

Indeed, in the race to being influential it may not be the most brilliant ideas that win, but the most transferable ones. As the saying goes, teach a man to fish and he will feed himself for ever; and nor is he likely to forget the person who taught him the lesson.

Our expertise starts to acquire a whole new audience the moment we start thinking of it as treasure to be shared rather than hoarded. What seems second nature to us, a skill or ability honed over a lifetime, will, I promise you, be coveted by somebody, somewhere. It's simply a matter of finding the sweet spot between our own areas of competence and an accessible audience willing to learn. Anyone can do it.

It is odd, then, that 'teaching' rarely crops up as a success criterion for many organizational roles outside the training department. You don't see it mentioned on appraisal forms. Maybe that's because the business of organizational learning has become something that has been outsourced to HR. Few of us outside academic circles would ever think of ourselves as teachers.

Yet whenever we possess a skill that others don't – and those others could be intimate colleagues or perfect strangers contemplating their smartphones on the other side of the world – an opportunity presents itself to become influential.

WRITE A HOW-TO GUIDE

If you were to start a blog – assuming you haven't done so already – you would soon get wise to one sure-fire way of attracting a little traffic. It's a tried and tested formula beloved of bloggers the world over, whether their field of expertise is quantum mechanics or brewing your own craft beer.

It's the how-to post, that easy-to-digest summary in five, seven or ten easy stages, that takes you through the process required to change a tyre, sail the Atlantic or make a million in a week. The how-to guide is a winner. Chances are it will get links and likes and get recycled and mashed up and get your name better known than any of the smarter posts you write that eschew the magic formula.

And this isn't just a phenomenon of the digital age. A certain title first published in 1936 has gone on to become one of the biggest selling non-fiction books of all time. Its name is *How to Win Friends and Influence People*.

This is why you need to author a how-to guide, whether your metier is online or the real world.

Beth, a junior executive at a global advertising agency, gained exposure this way, albeit unwittingly.

'We opened a lot of new offices a year or two ago and all of a sudden we had colleagues coming through London who didn't know the place. So I put together this little handout, just a two-page pdf, on how to make the most of your stay in the city. It was definitely lo-tech, just a few tongue-in-cheek recommendations of places to go and places to avoid. And wow, the impact this thing has had! I get emails on a weekly basis from all over the world, because our people have passed it on to their contacts outside the firm, saying "Just back from London and wanted you to know we used your guide and loved your recommendations…" The profile it has given me is incredible, and completely unexpected.'

Practical insight, pithily expressed: it's a winning formula.

🧩 SPONSOR, DESIGN OR FACILITATE A TRAINING PROGRAMME

The poor reputation of the training department of many organizations is puzzling. People often roll their eyes when training is mentioned, and there seems to be widespread cynicism about the impact training can make. Yet I look around me on the first morning of a new programme – particularly where new recruits are involved – and I don't see a lack of engagement. I see new faces and fresh minds that are at their most receptive.

Wouldn't you want to be in front of that crowd, positioning yourself as the go-to sage, influencing the talent that is likely to drive your share price in the years ahead? Unfortunately, it certainly doesn't seem to be on the list of priority tasks for most senior management, who consider themselves too busy to think about it.

The reason that training may have a bad reputation in some quarters is that organizations have experienced poor training. This has cast the many excellent trainers in the same bad light, but it is worth challenging this belief because the benefits of training can be enormous.

The urge to learn is still a strong one, whatever you may have read about Generation Y. Giving time and attention to what you want to teach people and how you are going to teach them is one of the most important investments you will make. Why not own it? Be the face of professional development in your organization. By all means partner with consultants – my favourite clients are those who share the stage with me at training events – but gain influence by getting known for taking other people's development seriously.

This is not just a corporate opportunity. The thirst for online information-based products is huge. Pat Flynn at Smart Passive Income publishes his monthly income online, and much of the $50,000 or so he makes each month comes from the sale of information-based products.

So, if you have some knowledge you can leverage, the development of some online products that gets your expertise out to the masses could generate influence – and income – while you sleep.

GIVE IT AWAY

Another early lesson that newbie bloggers learn is that content is king. The only way to build a loyal base of followers who keep coming back for more is to give them consistently high-quality, practical content that helps them achieve something they want to achieve. And, at the start at least, you give it away.

Brian Clark, the genius behind Copyblogger, ended up with a million-dollar business. He did it by building an audience who kept coming back for the high-quality content that he gave away on his site.

There are multiple ways of sharing your expertise online –
through commenting on blogs and discussions, joining groups
and answering questions.

By helping other people to solve their problems, by putting
your expertise at other people's disposal, you can begin to build
substantial online and real-world influence.

Putting it all together

Perhaps it's false modesty or perhaps it's a lack of awareness
but we seem reluctant to acknowledge that we know things
that other people don't, and that giving other people the
benefit of our experience or expertise isn't arrogant or
conceited but, done in the right way, incredibly empowering.

There is a twin benefit in using the teach approach to
building our influence. First, you get to showcase your
expertise. Second, you get to demonstrate your personal
values: you are committed to the development of other
people, which always seems a measure of integrity in those
who are serious about it.

Don't let the old saying about the world being divided into
doers and teachers put you off. The saying is out of date:
these days, those who *can*, teach.

- What how-to guide could you put together with the
  minimum of effort in the next hour? Who would find
  the information useful? How could you get them to
  see it?
- How involved are you in training within your
  organization?
- Do you have an information product you could
  develop for sale online? When did you last share your
  insight and expertise for someone else's gain?

9 Imagine

> 'What is now proved was once only imagined.' **William Blake**

> 'The function of the imagination is not to make strange things settled so much as to make settled things strange.' **G.K. Chesterton**

> 'Stay hungry. Stay foolish.' **Steve Jobs**

> 'The real act of discovery lies not in finding new lands but in seeing with new eyes.' **Marcel Proust**

> 'There are children playing in the street who could solve some of my top problems in physics, because they have modes of sensory perception that I lost long ago.' **J. Robert Oppenheimer**

John King, the director of a small creative agency based in London, has a special process for generating imaginative responses to clients' particularly onerous challenges.

'I turn it over first to the most junior member of the team. Literally, the intern or the new receptionist – I'm always interested in their take on it. When you need some really fresh thinking, you turn to those with the least experience because there's often a sort of naive brilliance in how they respond. It's sad in a way; you realize that the more experience you acquire, the more it gets in the way of fresh thinking.'

Some of the most frustrating moments in life are the 'blank page' episodes, when new thinking and fresh ideas are required but none seems to come. People who can get the ball rolling and 'unblock the pipe' are the ones who readily acquire influence in these situations. As John King suggests, this is often the preserve of the young. For children, a table can become a submarine, a darkened room a dragon's lair, in the blink of an eye. Somewhere along the road to adulthood, many of us lose that imaginative impulse, which was at the heart of Steve Jobs' lament in his famous Stanford commencement address. In his entreaty to his audience to 'stay foolish' was an appeal to retain some of the curiosity and imagination of a child. He of all people recognized that it is in the wildest leaps of the imagination that true greatness is to be found.

It is remarkable how few adults think of themselves as imaginative; even fewer would consider their imagination as a critical business tool that they need to take into work every day along with their mobile phones. In fact, it is relatively simple to find ways to unleash the imagination. One way is to encourage it in others: give others permission to think unconventionally. Another is to take heed of Einstein's famous definition of insanity: doing the same thing over and over again and expecting different results. Look for new ideas in different places. Open yourself up to fresh influences. In that way, the germ of an idea may appear to you that goes on to become an influential new approach, attitude or insight.

VARY THE FILTERS

We are creatures of habit, and while there is much comfort in the familiar it does not necessarily help provide a catalyst for the imagination or help us see things differently.

Varying sensory stimuli can sometimes be helpful. We work with groups who brainstorm using pictures instead of words, for example. One particularly productive session involved a team reaching consensus around an iceberg image to show that certain needs of their target market were being met by their current product range, but that there were many more latent possibilities than were currently being exploited. The key throughout the discussion was that people were required to *draw* their thoughts on a flipchart rather than write them. The session was huge fun, but it was also noticeable that individuals who might not contribute fully to a conventional meeting were much more 'present' with this approach.

Another manager, keen to ensure that the views of all his team were heard as the organization faced a period of upheaval, set his colleagues an unusual task. They were each told to write down some suggestions for change. Each of these mini scripts was then recorded by another team member, and the whole thing was issued as an mp3 file for the team to listen to at their leisure over the course of a week. There were two levels of unusual filtering here: the words were removed from their owners and also from interruptions and distractions. The views were appraised objectively and suggestions from unlikely sources ended up being wholeheartedly endorsed.

The chances of new ideas serendipitously emerging are greatly enhanced by varying the company you keep. Seek out new and unlikely collaborators within your own organization, or others.

'Marketing and finance never talk to each other' is the kind of comment we hear frequently. If you make it your business to bring new people into your meetings, or to seek an opinion from an outside source, the new perspective will refresh your own viewpoint and a more imaginative response may be the result.

BE A CATALYST

Influential people do not necessarily have to come up with all great ideas themselves. There is a category of influence that is all about creating the conditions in which others can prosper. It has an illustrious lineage: from the Medicis in Renaissance Florence and their patronage of the arts to the role of the Earl of Southampton in establishing Shakespeare as a dramatist, great creativity has often relied on a facilitator or benefactor to assist in its development.

In more contemporary terms, the role of producer in films and television is critical in relieving the artists of extraneous responsibilities, leaving them free to create. One of the most celebrated producers in British television was the late Bill Cotton, whom many of the great stars of TV and radio were keen to eulogize on his death. Here's Bruce Forsyth:

'Bill knew how to treat performers. He knew how to talk to them, how to get them to do things even if they didn't want to. He talked them into it because he knew it would be good for them.'

What, then, can you do to ensure that conditions are as advantageous as possible for your creative talent to prosper? Here is John King again:

'It's all about getting out of the way. Imaginative work cannot be micromanaged – as soon as you start imposing restrictions and asking for updates, you kill the creative process. I get the best out of our creative talent by being as "light touch" as I possibly can.'

WALK DOWN THE HIGH STREET NAKED

Sharing an imaginative thought with the world induces a feeling of incredible vulnerability. By its very nature, if you are proposing something completely different from prevailing norms, you have no sense of how it will be received. It might be loved or it might be vilified. You need to get used to this state. If you allow fear or self-consciousness to stifle you, your imaginative work will never see the light of day.

J.K. Rowling was famously rejected 12 times before getting her first manuscript accepted by a publisher. If she had retreated to her Edinburgh flat after the first rejection and thrown the manuscript in the bin, the world would never have been introduced to Harry Potter, and Rowling would never have been named the UK's most influential woman, as happened in 2010.

As one of John King's junior employees says:

'I do come up with a lot of ideas, and I generally have no clue which are good and which suck. So I just say what comes into my head. If it's a bad idea, that's fine: no one dies. But if it's a good one, that can really take us somewhere interesting.'

If you want to gain influence by proposing new, imaginative ideas, it is pointless doing what you always do and waiting for inspiration to strike. You need a process in place that will touch off unlikely associations, expose you to brand-new influences and then acquire the courage to launch your new thinking on the world.

And if you want to gain influence by shaping a team or organizational culture, finding a way to unleash people's creativity could be a very good place to start.

- How can you see things differently? Which senses do you underuse? Which people do you not tend to interact with?
- Who are the creatives in your team? What contribution do you make to ensuring that they have an environment conducive to creating?
- When did you last offer something original up for criticism? How did you feel? Will you do it again?

10 Disrupt

> 'Learn the rules like a pro, so you can break them like an artist.' Pablo Picasso

> 'In times of widespread chaos and confusion, it has been the duty of more advanced human beings – artists, scientists, clowns and philosophers – to create order. In times such as ours, however, when there is too much order, too much management, too much programming and control, it becomes the duty of superior men and women to fling their favourite monkey wrenches into the machinery. To relieve the repression of the human spirit, they must sow doubt and disruption.' Tom Robbins

> 'Undermine their pompous authority, reject their moral standards, make anarchy and disorder your trademarks. Cause as much chaos and disruption as possible but don't let them take you ALIVE.' Sid Vicious

> 'If I'd observed all the rules, I'd never have got anywhere.' Marilyn Monroe

> 'True disruption means threatening your existing product line and your past investments. Breakthrough products disrupt current lines of businesses.' Peter Diamandis

As the old saying reminds us, to make a soufflé you need to break some eggs.

Serial disrupters are those kinds of people for whom it's anything but business as usual. Disruption is a potent mix of the creative and the destructive, and it is a high-risk influencing tactic because it takes on vested interests with impunity. Don't choose this approach if you want everyone to love you. However, the rewards are commensurate with the risk: it's the game changers who often clean up.

Disruption is different from innovation because it involves an element of shock: old ways of doing things are violently uprooted and something radically different is installed in their place. The classic example of this is, of course, Apple and the transformation it wrought in the music business with the iPod.

Historically, it has been creative artists who have been the greatest disrupters. Compare and contrast the work of Pablo Picasso at the beginning and the end of the first decade of the twentieth century and you will find an extraordinary transformation from traditional, representational figure painting to the wilder excesses of Cubism. Likewise, if you listen to Bob Dylan's first album and then immediately afterwards listen to *Blonde on Blonde,* released a mere four years later, you will hear the evidence of an extraordinary musical journey. When Dylan went 'electric' in 1966, he left behind his initial audience of folk aficionados; his response, when the old audience hooted with derision as he plugged in his electric guitar, was to tell his band to 'play it f****** loud'. Similarly, the Sex Pistols were about as disruptive as it was possible to be given the nature of the pop charts in 1977 – and their influence went on to extend to bands emerging almost four decades later.

Disruption is all about stating uncomfortable truths, breaking taboos and disturbing people out of their complacency. Eve Ensler, author of the controversial play *The Vagina Monologues,* expresses it like this: 'It's that beautiful cutting edge, where people are disturbed enough to start thinking about things.'

Essential requirements for would-be disrupters therefore include a thick skin and a tin hat. And if you weather the short-term flak, your longer-term prospects might start looking up.

LEARN THE ROPES

To stand a chance of getting your disruptive idea off the ground, you need to have a thorough understanding of the way things work at the moment. There is a widely held myth that the only opportunity one has to bring about significant change is right at the beginning of a project, job or opportunity – the so-called '100 Days' strategy of disruptive change. In fact, if you try to disrupt the status quo before fully understanding it, you will create enough resentment to ensure that your idea will never get implemented.

An experienced CEO in the not-for-profit sector told us:

'The first thing you need to do when you start a new role or join an organization is look, listen and learn. You can't go in and start changing things immediately because you don't know where the power lies, what the risk appetite is, what people's motivations are. So sit in and see how the land lies.'

Likewise, in the virtual world, the one thing guaranteed to annoy the members of a discussion group or forum is the newbie who comes in and starts wanting to change things. It is therefore important to get used to the key participants and the tone of the interactions first, and begin with some small contributions. Once you have built up some relationships, people will have grown to trust and like you; once you have enough knowledge of the status quo that you can critique it with authority, then, and only then, are you in a position to advance.

TAKE OWNERSHIP

There are many reasons why people may not jump up and down with unrestrained enthusiasm when you suggest a major change or disruption. High on the list of responses would be envy, inertia and cynicism, but at the top of the list would be simple fear.

What you are proposing is new; you are asking people to enter unchartered territory. The natural reaction of those around you runs something like this:

- 'It sounds risky.'
- 'We have no means of guaranteeing success.'

- 'Failure could have serious consequences to our career prospects.'
- 'Let's block it.'

The way to circumvent this type of resistance is by making it clear that you will take full responsibility for the new initiative. If it fails, it will be your reputation on the line, no one else's.

Here is the CEO again:

'People are understandably protective of their reputations, so if you want their support or their involvement you have to be protective of their reputations, too. Ask people to help you here and there, surreptitiously. Promise them a share of the limelight if it works, but a get-out-of-jail card if it flounders.'

If you wait for permission to implement your disruption, or for consensus around it, you are destined for disappointment. Neutrality – a lack of vociferous opposition – is probably the best you can hope for, and that is best achieved by assuming full responsibility for the new direction. Everyone else can look from the safety of the shadows until they feel it is safe to hitch themselves publicly to your wagon.

GET STARTED

If you need the involvement of other people to get your idea off the ground and the idea is genuinely disruptive in nature, be prepared for many rounds of knockbacks. People will find any excuse they can to say no.

Your response to this should be to try to begin the process of change, however small that first step might be. (Think of Jobs and Wozniack in their garage.) The key is to make the idea tangible and then keep going back to other people with the results of your labours.

Susie, an event planner, was having little luck persuading a local authority to close down all the key streets in a large town for a midsummer arts festival. So, in her own time, she went about the business of getting mock-ups made; she filmed interviews with local residents about how they would feel about such an event; every time she had a meeting with the authority – often about other matters – she would introduce another piece of 'collateral' to demonstrate that the festival idea already had a head of steam.

'After the third or fourth meeting, the mood changed from "This is ridiculous, it simply won't work," to "This looks fantastic, can't wait to see it." You have to remember that the biggest impediment to getting new projects off the ground is other people's lack of imagination. They often just don't see it. They need help to see it in concrete terms – you just have to start transforming your vision into reality and accept that a lot of people won't buy in till quite a late stage.'

Putting it all together

Disruption, then, is not safe; it involves the complete overhaul of the existing order. Vested interests will be vociferous in their opposition. You may have to extend your timeframe again and again. But those who are successful at bringing about a disruption – think of the damage the jet aircraft did to the steamship, or the flash drive to the floppy disk – may create a whole new market.

- Is your market ripe for disruption?
- How well do you know the environment you want to disrupt?
- Can you start small? If you are not a 'disrupter' yourself, can you encourage it in others?

11 Specialize

'Be faithful to that which exists nowhere but in yourself – and thus make yourself indispensable.' André Gide

'Every man has a specific skill, whether it is discovered or not, that more readily and naturally comes to him than it would to another, and his own should be sought and polished. He excels best in his niche – originality loses its authenticity in one's efforts to obtain originality.' Criss Jami

'An expert is someone who has succeeded in making decisions and judgements simpler through knowing what to pay attention to and what to ignore.' Edward de Bono

'An investment in knowledge pays the best interest.'
Benjamin Franklin

'The illiterate of the 21st century will not be those who cannot read and write, but those who cannot learn, unlearn, and relearn.' Alvin Toffler

It is easy for people to thing that they are an expert these days. Thanks to the Internet, doctors' surgeries are full of people who have Googled their symptoms so exhaustively that they think they know more than the doctor. Parents tell teachers what they've read about the latest educational fad, and how it should be immediately adopted to benefit their offspring. For years now, people have been predicting the end of lawyers because their stock-in-trade – the law – is so easily accessed and processed by the punter at his home computer. Why bother to pay a professional to read what you can read for yourself?

However, amateurs have not displaced the professionals. A basic level of information is not expertise. Doctors, lawyers and teachers are not going out of business. Perhaps, as the man or woman in the street explores the tip of the informational iceberg, he or she has a greater respect for the immensity of the unknown that lies beneath.

Just as it is true that breadth of knowledge is easier to come by than ever before, true depth of knowledge remains elusive. Our attention spans are shortening, so the endeavour required to achieve true expertise looks increasingly daunting. And this presents an opportunity for the would-be influential.

Generalists are an endangered species. Know a little bit about something, and the 'neterati' are coming to get you. Know a lot – the kind of knowledge you can acquire only through years of patient study rather than half an hour's surfing – about something very specific and you can become the 'go-to' person.

Turning yourself into an 'expert' could be one of the smartest moves you make. You differentiate yourself immediately from the crowd and, if you select your specialism carefully, you can become the voice or the face of a particular subject, always in demand.

SPECIALIZE IN SOMETHING UNFASHIONABLE

The key to specialization as a strategy for bringing you influence is that you need to develop intellectual capital that is in high demand but short supply. The second part is crucial; there is no point in selecting specialist turf and then finding that you are in competition with many others. To give you a return on the investment of time and effort it takes to become a specialist, you must have the field largely to yourself. This means avoiding fads, trends and fashionable areas of activity.

A tax lawyer explains how he went about the process of specializing:

'When I joined the firm as a trainee in the mid-2000s, everybody wanted to be a capital markets lawyer. It was where the really sexy stuff was happening. The derivatives partners were the masters of the universe. Everyone wanted to qualify into their teams, to become the next capital markets sensation. But I remember thinking about this quite clearly: I didn't want to be part of that crowd. I'm quite nerdy really, and figures and proper full-on intellectual challenge really appeal to me. So I chose tax as my area, because I figured it was a good fit for my personality and also, though unfashionable at the time, tax is always going to be with us so I thought it had a sort of long-term viability."

While betting your future on an area of specialization is clearly a bit of a gamble, some basic principles are at work here, which you can apply to limit the risk. Is your area of specialization addressing a need for which people will always be willing to pay: for health, wealth or an easy life, for example? Then look at the barriers for entry to that area of specialization. Low barriers mean high competition: look at the plethora of life coaches out there. They address a need certainly – for people who need a little help with the direction of their lives. But because anyone can set themself up as a life coach, competition is plentiful and it would be very difficult to claim the 'life coaching' space for your own.

But tax law – or cranial osteopathy or the ability to customize vintage Harley Davidsons? This is intellectual capital that requires a serious investment of time and money, so competition will be manageable. But they are good bets for specialization: people will always want to avoid the taxman, soothe their babies' cries or spend their way out of a mid-life crisis.

BUILD YOUR INTELLECTUAL CAPITAL – CONTINUOUSLY

So you've decided on an area of specialization, maybe taken a course and got some qualifications. Job done, right? Wrong. The process of updating your skillset or knowledge is never-ending. Obsolescence is one of the curses of the digital age: new ideas or adaptations that once would have taken an age to migrate from country to country can now circle the globe in the click of a mouse. If you are serious about protecting your specialist territory, you will need to make a lifelong commitment to keeping your knowledge up to date.

Let's return to our tax lawyer:

'I'd been working a few years and I had a good, but not market-leading, practice. If I wanted to make the next leap, to become part of the tax law elite, I knew I had to invest again in my knowledge base. I knew that a change to tax law was being considered by the government, so I arranged to go on secondment to HMRC [the UK's tax-collection body]. People thought I was mad because I would be out of the office. But I was there when the implications of the new legislation were being considered on the inside, and the knowledge I acquired there differentiated me from the competition so that, on this new change, I became the go-to person. I had acquired, if you like, 'specialized' specialist knowledge.'

❸ LEARN TO COMMUNICATE YOUR SPECIALISM IN PLAIN ENGLISH

Expertise without visibility is no recipe for influence. Having the knowledge or the skills is only part of the story – you have to be able to communicate it to the market. There is a paradox here; experts who become truly influential are often those who can demythologize technical areas, step back from their specialism and discuss it in language understandable by all. The pundits picked up by TV stations to discuss economics, say, or scientific discoveries are experts of a particular kind: they are subject-matter experts but great communicators, too.

Unless you are an academic, it is unlikely that you will spend your time discussing your specialist area with your peer group. If you are going to make your living through selling a specialism, by definition, you have to be able to communicate its value. Essentially, having learned your trade, you need to unlearn or, at least, deconstruct it.

A final word from our tax lawyer:

'While I am a nerd, I don't talk like one. My colleagues in other departments know that, if they have a tax query, they can call me and I will give them a view in plain English. There's no point in being a specialist if all you do is intimidate or confuse people. The key is to be useful – and approachable.'

Developing a specialism takes time, effort and sometimes also major investment, but there is undoubted potential for gaining influence through specialized knowledge. The old saw was wrong – it's both who you know *and* what you know that counts.

You should consider several factors before deciding what to specialize in:

- Can you develop a specialism that will have long-term viability?
- Is it in a field that is not too competitive so that your expertise will have scarcity value?
- Can you commit to continual self-renewal?

12 Synthesize

> '' 'We need to look at the subtle, the hidden, and the unspoken.'
> Malcolm Gladwell

> '' 'With the Dual Cyclone's see-through bin, everyone said it
> would never sell. People did not want to look at the crap they
> had sucked out of the carpet... But the very disadvantage is
> what gives it its magic. People look at it and say, "My God, it
> works!"' James Dyson

> '' 'You can't connect the dots looking forward; you can only
> connect them looking backwards. So you have to trust that
> the dots will somehow connect in your future. You have to
> trust in something – your gut, destiny, life, karma, whatever.
> This approach has never let me down, and it has made all the
> difference in my life.' Steve Jobs

> '' 'I believe in connections between the players. I think what
> makes football great is that it is a team sport. You can win in
> different ways, by being more of a team, or by having better
> individual players. It is the team ethic that interests me,
> always.' Arsene Wenger

> '' Watson: 'I can see nothing.'
> Holmes: 'On the contrary, Watson, you can see everything. You
> fail, however, to reason from what you see. You are too timid in
> drawing your inferences.' Arthur Conan Doyle, 'The Adventure of the
> Blue Carbuncle'

Influence is immediately bestowed on the innovators. We romanticize our pioneers, inventors and creatives, putting their pictures on our banknotes and their statues on real or metaphorical pedestals. Because of this, we may think that the art of fresh thinking lies beyond our reach, the domain of a few natural-born geniuses. How on earth can the rest of us hope to enlist innovation as a tool to increase our influence?

On closer examination, however, the process of innovation becomes a little less intimidating. Rarely does fresh, insightful thinking emerge like a rabbit pulled from a magician's hat or a bolt from the blue. Instead, it's more often a process of joining the dots, of intuiting connections between people or things that have been staring you in the face for years. The secret lies in opening your eyes to patterns and connections that already exist but that no one has noticed.

There are three stages to deploying innovation or fresh thinking as a means of increasing influence:

1. Identify a specific problem that needs solving.
2. Consider the resources already at your disposal: can they be reconfigured, juxtaposed or otherwise manipulated to fashion a solution?
3. Put your head above the parapet and make your suggestion.

The final stage is the most challenging. It is very easy, particularly in large organizations, to avoid fresh thinking and carry on making the same old mistakes simply because that's the way it has always been done around here. It takes guts to challenge the status quo, so all too often great ideas go begging. But before dismissing your new idea on the grounds that it is too simple, or too obvious, or too unlikely to receive anyone else's support, why not voice it?

There's every chance that your colleagues may see you afresh – as a visionary, an innovator or even a genius!

LEVERAGE EXISTING MARKETS

Simon Cowell's big break was not *X Factor* or even *Pop Idol*. Rather, it came in 1995 when he realized that the audience for a hit TV show (in this case, the UK drama *Soldier, Soldier*) could be induced to buy songs recorded by the show's stars in vast numbers. Whatever your take on Robson & Jerome's version of 'Unchained Melody', there is no denying that it sold more than 3 million copies.

The secret of Cowell's success was not that he was brilliantly creative: the song was a 40-year-old standard, the singers were, by their own admission, average at best. Instead, the success of the project lay in making a new connection: between a hit TV show and the music business.

Existing clients, customers and contacts are always more valuable than new ones because, having bought once, they are more likely to buy again. What new product or service could you offer to your existing fans that could help boost your market share, profitability or chances of promotion?

RECYCLE EXISTING SOLUTIONS

James Dyson may have changed the way we clean our homes, but his first successful invention was intended for use in the garden. The 'Ballbarrow' was a reinvention of the wheelbarrow and it enjoyed modest success in the late 1970s. As part of the production process, Dyson needed to find a way of unclogging the air filter in the Ballbarrow paint room. This he did by means of an industrial cyclone tower, which removed the paint particles from the air via centrifugal force. So far, so boring, right?

It was only when the inventor was subsequently troubled by a vacuum cleaner that wasn't up to the job that the cyclone tower assumed a greater significance. Perhaps the principle of centrifugal force could be applied to the way we remove dust from our carpets?

Again, it is important (and heartening) to note that success here didn't come from pure invention. Centrifugal force had been discovered in the mid-seventeenth century. The smart bit was in the application of an existing solution to an apparently unrelated existing problem.

It's surprising how solutions to problems sometimes emerge just by shifting our perspective. We have a problem at work, say. How would we handle a similar problem at home? What would Richard Branson do, or Mickey Mouse? When did we last encounter a similar problem, and what did we do then?

SHUFFLE THE PACK

It isn't easy being an Arsenal supporter. At the time of writing, the north London football club has gone eight long seasons without a trophy. Astonishingly, in a game renowned for its ruthless treatment of managers who don't acquire the silverware, manager Arsene Wenger has remained in charge at Arsenal throughout. He is one of the most influential football managers in the world. How has he done it?

The answer is by doing more with less. With a fraction of the spending power of the monster Premier League clubs, Wenger has secured champions league qualification in every one of the last 16 seasons. He spends frugally, and often unexpectedly. He puts a lot of faith in young talent spotted early. He ignores the calls from the media and sometimes the fans to emulate other clubs, to go for the glamorous signing. He tinkers with what he's got. And the record, while not stellar, is amazingly consistent.

Sometimes, the whole dynamic of a team, a project or a career can be transformed by juggling the personnel. Pair up people who are not used to working with each other. Take for yourself a task that you've hitherto avoided. Instead of dreaming about hiring that transformational striker, maybe tinker with the defence instead.

Coming up with a smart idea never did anyone's career any harm. And, as this chapter has shown, you don't have to be Einstein to come up with some fresh thinking. Some of the most influential people around today got there because they had their eyes and ears open to connections, patterns and possibilities that nobody else registered.

Putting it all together

Having the idea is one thing. Launching it on the world is another. Practise making some suggestions: 'What if…?' 'How about…?' 'This is probably nothing new but…' You may be surprised at how seriously you are taken for simply saying what was obvious to you all along.

- Can you transfer a technique that has brought you success from one area of life to another?
- Could the same people be even more effective in different roles?
- Where could you stand, metaphorically, to get a new perspective?

Part 2

Who you know: influence through interactions

13　Be the bridge

> ❝ *'I have a respect for manners as such, they are a way of dealing with people you don't agree with or like.'* Margaret Mead

> ❝ *'Golden bridge, silver bridge or diamond bridge; it doesn't matter! As long as the bridge takes you across the other side, it is a good bridge!'* Mehmet Murat Ildan

> ❝ *'A simple rule in dealing with those who are hard to get along with is to remember that this person is striving to assert his superiority; and you must deal with him from that point of view.'* Alfred Adler

> ❝ *'People fail to get along because they fear each other; they fear each other because they don't know each other; they don't know each other because they have not communicated with each other.'* Martin Luther King Jr.

East or west, old or young, town or country, coffee or tea: where do you sit? Which side of the divide are you on?

There are so many of them: cultural, generational or divisions that are merely the product of a marketing man's mercurial mind. The more we define ourselves in this binary way, the greater the inherent danger. What starts off as a preference can harden into a prejudice – we associate ourselves so completely with one product or attitude or camp that we struggle to see anything positive on the other side. This is not such a problem at the level of choosing a product such as a computer, but when those divides reach schism proportions between teams, organizations or even countries, there is an issue.

However, this also presents an opportunity. Anyone who can bridge the divide – act as an interpreter or a mediator between factions – will obtain a position of unique influence. The go-between, an individual with an ability to keep an open mind, understand both sides and with the tenacity to work tirelessly to bring them together, can transform any arena, from international relations to a playground stand-off.

'Bridging' can, of course, settle or resolve disputes. But it can also promote funky experimentation. The language of 'both… and…' rather than 'either… or…' has been responsible for some great success stories in recent years. Consider the automobile market: a few years ago, you would have had to choose *either* an SUV *or* a passenger sedan. They were distinct and separate categories. Now you can buy both in one vehicle: the 'crossover' dominates the industry – it combines the best features of two automobile segments with relatively small concessions to each – and for manufacturers such as Lexus, their crossover models are now their most popular.

In politics, too, the most electorally successful individuals have appealed not only to their natural support base. Leaders from Thatcher to Obama owed their victories to their ability to appeal directly to their *opponent's* supporters, often to the chagrin of the party faithful. They were crossover politicians, able to bridge the electoral divide – and therefore secure margins of victory that eluded more partisan contenders.

KEEP A FOOT IN BOTH CAMPS

A recent *New York Times* article profiled Melvin Lim, the man who occupies a hugely influential role in the worlds of fashion and retail by 'arranging a match between the world's most prestigious luxury brands and the world's fastest-growing consumer market'. Lim is essentially a go-between, a hugely successful entrepreneur who has made his fortune by helping Western brands ease their way into the Chinese market, and Chinese stars make it big in the West. He doesn't make or market anything himself. His skill is as a cross-cultural facilitator, enabling commercial interaction between two cultures by understanding both, and as a result is big in both East and West.

Having a foot in both camps can be a very smart move, even at a less rarefied level. So many organizations are in silos; the team on floor 4 doesn't know what's going on up on floor 5. Marketing doesn't speak to IT. It's not animus necessarily, just ignorance. So what if you become the person who acts as the bridge? Start a conversation across offices, functions and divisions, for no other motive than curiosity. The reward may be that you can start to open up new channels of communication and become the interlocutor of choice. You get to be invited to both sets of meetings. If the two sides need to collaborate, they will probably rely on you to get it done.

A CFO of an Asian-based multinational put it this way:

'I have to be the arbiter between the boardroom and operations. One of our business units may request new investment, which the board might normally dismiss. A stand-off could occur, so I need to explain the operational considerations to the board and the strategic imperatives to the business units. I am responsible for that dialogue – views can be expressed through me that would not be accepted if heard direct from the other side.'

Be the conduit, the messenger, and become influential to all sides, not just your own.

MASH IT UP

Steve Jobs didn't invent the mobile phone, or email, or portable music. But he did make the game-changing decision to bring them all together on one device.

Uber-cool dance duo Daft Punk alienated some hardcore fans with their smash-hit album *Random Access Memories*: it contained a melange of styles ranging from the disco-inspired 'Get Lucky' to lush seventies balladry. Why did they change gear? The duo made the point that they had always been interested in different eras and different styles and bringing them together on one album helped achieve their objective of 'a certain timelessness'.

This is, of course, the age of the 'mash-up' – where disparate elements in music or technology are brought together to make something new, better or just different. What can you combine? Processes, roles or work spaces? New ingredients for supper?

The potential for 'crossover' is everywhere; we just need to adjust our tunnel vision to look for it. You can establish whole new markets and new opportunities by finding common ground where previously people thought there was none.

ACT AS PEACEMAKER

One of the most gifted – and occasionally controversial – US diplomats of the post-war period was Richard Holbrooke. He was one of the main players in brokering the Dayton Peace Accords that ended the war in Bosnia in 1995, and went on, with less success, to become President Obama's special representative for Afghanistan and Pakistan. He was known to be that rare thing: a diplomat with real clout.

Another senior diplomat who had watched Holbrooke at close quarters gave me this analysis of his modus operandi:

'He had the willingness to put in the 98-per-cent perspiration. He would telephone a hundred people if necessary. He would talk to unsympathetic people, often keeping a channel of communication open to them when no one else would, just to ensure they wouldn't foul things up. He really worked at it.'

Acting as peacemaker is not for the faint-hearted but will help you gain influence.

Dispute resolution is painstaking work, which is why so many disputes go unresolved. There is, however, always an opportunity to assume the role of peacemaker. If you feel you can help to mediate between warring factions – at work or at home – it is probably as well to be prepared for the long haul. And it may mean you having to give time and attention to views you find objectionable. It is also unlikely that you will gain much credit: when disputes are resolved, the antagonists win the laurels rather than the mediators who facilitated the process.

Yet, even if you don't win public recognition, you will gain influence. Helping to unblock a communication channel may not be glamorous work, but having helped end the war you will almost certainly have a critical role in maintaining the peace.

Putting it all together

Contemporary life seems to put people in ever more granular categories – if we are not X, then we must be Y. There is a real opportunity here for an influencer: you can be the visionary who sees the shades of grey as opposed to the black and white, or the mediator who gets the opposing factions talking to each other.

- Where can you be the go-between, the conduit? Do you know people who would benefit from closer alignment? Take responsibility for explaining and interpreting disconnected entities to each other, and for exploring common ground.
- How can you combine two existing categories to make an exciting, innovative third? What opportunities for crossovers are there, or for increased collaboration?
- Where are the stand-offs in your life – both at work and at home? Do you have the patience, resilience and tenacity to mediate?

14 Adapt to connect

CC 'You must constantly change and adapt to a new environment.'
Jong-Yong Yun

CC 'We are all multidimensional and kind of have dual personalities. Everyone puts on different roles depending on what circumstances they're in without even noticing that they do that.' Carla Gugino

CC 'A flexible team member can consider different points of views and compromise when needed. He or she doesn't hold rigidly to a point of view and argue it to death, especially when the team needs to move forward to make a decision or get something done.' Marty Brounstein

CC 'When you adapt your style to others, it will help you build much better bridges to them. They will respect your approach (because, after all, it's like theirs). They will trust you more. They will think more highly of you.' Susan Cullen

'Authenticity' was an in-vogue word a few years ago. People were encouraged to put their 'true selves' on show, warts and all. The self was immutable, fixed, beyond reproach, and anyone who didn't respond favourably to the authentic self you had to show them frankly wasn't worth concerning yourself with.

There are several problems with this approach. You effectively limit your sphere of influence to people who are exactly like you, or immediately disposed to liking you. Secondly, in concerning yourself exclusively with who you are and how you want to be

70

perceived, you miss all the subtle cues coming from other people that might help you connect more effectively with them.

Great influencers tend to be fascinated readers of other people's personalities, foibles and motivations. They spend time working out what makes other people tick. And, armed with this intelligence, they turn chameleon; they find a way of connecting that is entirely consistent with the other person's preferences. If the other person is a culture vulture, they would realize that tickets to the football match would be of limited interest. The opera, though, might be a different story... And if they are dealing with someone with little capacity or inclination for small talk, they would be unlikely to risk their wrath by giving them a blow-by-blow account of their latest holiday. It would be straight down to business.

Flexing our approach to suit other people isn't compromising or manipulative, it's just a short cut to getting a functioning relationship up and running. The alternative – ignoring the signals you get from other people and subscribing to the mantra 'What you see is what you get, take me or leave me' – is at best deluded, at worst crassly antisocial.

The old saw is wrong – to influence effectively, don't treat others as you wish to be treated yourself; treat them as they wish to be treated.

REMEMBER: DIFFERENT STROKES FOR DIFFERENT FOLKS

Personality profiling is big business these days, with a multitude of tools and assessments available to categorize your behavioural preferences. There is one dimension that seems to be common to all the approaches, however – the spectrum of extraversion/ introversion. You will see this spectrum at work every day: in meetings, for example, there will be those whose contributions burst forth like a river and others who say barely a word. Recognizing the difference is only the first step – you will need to adopt completely different communication styles to get the best out of these interactions.

- **Extroverts** get their stimulation from the outside world – they will be in their element talking, arguing and brainstorming. Provocative questioning and challenge are likely to get the best out of them.

- **Introverts** – as Susan Cain has documented in her fine book *Quiet* – get their energy from within, so they need patient drawing out with plenty of time allowed them for reflection.

Getting this wrong – particularly if, as an extrovert yourself, you project this preference indiscriminately on to others and misinterpret reflectiveness as disinterest – can mean that you will never connect with certain individuals and influencing them will be an uphill task.

UNDERSTAND OTHER PEOPLE'S 'CURRENCY'

Just as people's personality styles vary, so does their fundamental motivation. For some, money is the key driver. For others, it is recognition. Another group hankers after variety in life, or more discretionary time. Understanding this – getting the exact 'currency' those around you most value – is the key to leverage in influencing situations.

Paul, an experienced manager in a financial services company, acknowledges that he has made mistakes in this area:

'Money talks for me, always has. That's why I thrive in a bonus culture – if extra effort is rewarded by better remuneration, that's motivating for me. But I made the mistake of thinking everyone was the same – saying, come on, stay late tonight and there's a few quid in it for you. And one day one colleague said: "If we could have a conversation about how I could earn less, but get out of here on time every night, that's how you are going to get the best out of me." And it clicked: home life mattered more than bank balance, and so I totally changed the way I managed him.'

And just as the currency itself will vary, so will the way in which it is used. As any sports coach will testify, some players respond best to an arm around the shoulder, others to a kick up the backside. Whether you incentivize by promising more of a valued currency, or by threatening to reduce what they already have, is a key judgement to make.

COMMUNICATE THEIR WAY

Our own communication preferences are often surprisingly hard-wired. We prefer email or we prefer SMS. We write long, flowing sentences or we prefer pithy bullet points. We like the slow, rational exposition of an argument, showing exactly how we reached our conclusions, or we cut straight to the chase.

Learning how colleagues and stakeholders like their information provides a real head start in terms of influencing them, but few people even contemplate this sort of flexibility. So the lawyer who constructs a meticulous five-page draft fails to understand the irritation of the busy client who only ever reads what can be viewed on a single scroll of the Blackberry screen. The twenty-something IT specialist who responds to queries with one-line texts doesn't appreciate an older generation who despair and say: 'Why can't he just pick up the phone?'

Selecting the favoured communication channel is important; so, too, is recognizing the difference between 'big picture' operators and 'read the small print' merchants. Get this wrong, and it won't matter how great your argument is because it will never be read.

Putting it all together

Influencing would be simple if everyone functioned exactly the way we do – liked the same food, made decisions the same way, responded to stress in identical fashion. The trap of similarity, particularly when dealing with people superficially akin to us, in age, say, or cultural background, is alluring – and highly dangerous.

If we are to connect effectively, we must suspend all assumptions about how others function until we have spent the time and trouble really getting to know them. Then it is a question of flexibility: do we have the capacity to give them what they want in the way they want it?

If you've even been cornered by the office bore at a social function, you'll know how uncomfortable it is to be forced to listen as he talks about himself and his life in microscopic detail. You run the risk of causing similar discomfort if you fail to adapt your approach to the style of the recipient. One note grates after a while. You need to change key to stay easy on the ear.

- What key differences do you notice in the styles of people you live and work with?
- How sure are you about the motivators of your staff?
- How can you flex your communication style to connect more effectively with different styles?

15 Build – then nurture – a tribe

> 'The richest people in the world look for and build networks, everyone else looks for work.' Robert Kiyosaki

> 'It's all about people. It's about networking and being nice to people and not burning any bridges.' Mike Davidson

> 'The true test of a leader is whether his followers will adhere to his cause from their own volition, enduring the most arduous hardships without being forced to do so, and remaining steadfast in the moments of greatest peril.' Xenophon

> 'Call it a clan, call it a network, call it a tribe, call it a family. Whatever you call it, whoever you are, you need one.' Jane Howard

Influence grows best by third-party referral. While self-promotion has its place, done badly it comes off as nakedly self-aggrandizing. The influential down the years have always relied on their proxies and spokespersons to spread the word. From the great religions to the latest tech trend, it's the small band of early adopters and true believers who make the difference between an idea that spreads and one that is stillborn. It's the principle of social proof in action: if six people find your views insightful, and those six pass word to their mates... pretty soon a little gang becomes a large crowd. So creating your own tribe, a band of loyal followers bound together by their passion for an idea or common interest (not loyalty to you – that would seem dangerously cultish), is a powerful way of gaining influence.

The trouble is that followers need leading, nurturing and sustaining. While this may seem self-evident, still the mantle of 'leadership' sits uneasily on the shoulders of many would-be influencers. They hope the brilliance of their thinking alone will win them the loyalty of adoring fans, who will then go off unaided and promulgate the message to the masses. Needless to say, this is a strategy based on luck rather than judgement.

You need to attract your tribe in the first place. It could be a common interest, it could be a sparkling vision of the future: whatever it is, you have to believe that you and your idea are worth following. Some people never get to this stage, which is why the cures for cancer and global warming are probably already out there but have yet to benefit the rest of us because their originators lack a crucial attribute: the self-belief to launch their idea upon the world.

Daniel, a successful blogger with a large and loyal following, makes this point:

'It takes guts to put yourself out there in the first place, to get your message out of your head and into the public arena. Then, when one or two people respond, agree with you, like what you say, that's an amazing moment. But that's also a critical moment, when you need to step up and lead and nurture and build a community. Your work isn't over when you get followers. That's when it really starts.'

ADDRESS A BASIC, UNMET NEED

To gain any traction, your proposition will need to appeal to a basic need in your target audience. Social scientist Clayton Alderfer, building on the earlier work of Abraham Maslow, categorized the basic needs as existence, relatedness and growth. His work provides a useful checklist for your tribe-building proposition: does it help people thrive, interact or develop their capabilities?

Helping people thrive means attending to the basics of health, wealth and happiness. Offer assistance in any of these areas and you at least catch people's attention. Take 'consumer champion' Martin Lewis, who started one of the UK's most popular websites. Its title tells you everything about his proposition and why it was so successful that he eventually sold it for £87 million: Money Saving Expert. Click on the site and you get access to a multitude of money-saving tips and hints, most of them saving you a few pence; but the proposition aligns with that basic need to save money and maximize resources.

The sites above MSE in the rankings are mostly social networking forums, which points up our need to hang out with other people, whether in the real world or the virtual one. But you don't need a Facebook-rivalling platform to facilitate this kind of community interaction. The beauty of the Internet is that it presents an opportunity for relatively small groups of enthusiasts to gather and confer. Enjoy restoring vintage Cadillacs? There are clubs for that. Starting out in Malaysian cookery? There are clubs for that. If you define and parse your audience precisely enough, and hit that sweet spot of pressing need to interact with few opportunities to do so – again, you stand a chance of building a tribe.

Finally, there is the market for personal development, or learning. MOOCs (massive open online courses) are set to revolutionize further education. They offer the prospect of personal or professional development at negligible cost, and tens of thousands of willing students sign up. Does your proposition help people build or develop a skill, or gain important new knowledge?

BUILD AND NURTURE YOUR TRIBE

Like any relationship, the key to ensuring that your tribe has a viable future is effort. Whether your tribe is real or virtual, you will need to take responsibility for co-ordinating its activity. Arranging venues, reminding people of dates and times, posting new content for discussion and commentary, these are the maintenance tasks you will need to undertake if your tribe is to survive and flourish.

Above all, it is your job as an influencer to make 'membership' fun. Encourage spiky observations, ask provocative questions, vary the venue, communicate with the members bilaterally, asking for their views or thanking them for a previous contribution.

A recruitment consultant told me this story about building a tribe:

'We took on about six people all at the same time, all in the 25–30 age range. And I thought, I'm going to build a little powerhouse here. I'm going to forge a community identity, we're going to push each other to deliver the best, and we are going to become the highest-earning division in the business. We called ourselves the A team, used to go out for a pizza every Monday night, occasionally got together with families at the weekend. And the performance of that team was – for about a year – phenomenal. Of course, there were adverse comments from other parts of the business – that's the thing with a high-performing team, people outside feel they are missing out, that's inevitable – but I just wanted this team of kids to really gel and really produce. And for a time they did. Then people move on and the enthusiasm dimmed, but for a while there, this community was really tight and achieved a performance we could not have done without that level of interdependence and ritual, almost…'

GROW – OR GO

Tribes are not cliques; if they are not to grow stale, they need to be in a constant state of renewal. Nor do tribes need to be permanent. Increasingly, groups of people come together to achieve a specific objective and then they disband as soon as that objective is achieved.

Sometimes, though, the danger with building a successful tribe is that it becomes all consuming and intoxicating. The tribe is seen as an end rather than the means.

Influence deriving from your position as tribe leader is many-sided. You find yourself at the centre of the conversation. People begin to rely on your co-ordination. As convenor, there is little you do not hear about. Your ideas may gain a ready audience, and if the tribe achieves critical mass it may win you wider attention in your organization, locality or even around the world. But does the exposure justify the workload? This is the moment when, as tribe leader, you face an important question: to grow or go?

Alan, a manager in one of the world's largest consumer goods manufacturers, highlights the dilemma:

'I built a project team to deliver a new product line. We were enthusiasts, evangelists almost. There was a big bonding element to it, we met regularly, we were in constant email communication. We almost began to see the rest of the organization as the enemy: non-believers who we were out to convert. And it worked. It was the most successful implementation of its kind. I got a lot of exposure at senior levels, because I was the leader of this thing. The trouble is that a group like that starts to make a big demand on your time – people become quite needy. So I disbanded it, probably about three months later than I should have done.'

Putting it all together

If you want to be seen as influential, why not get yourself a band of followers? The idea may sound preposterous, but don't underestimate the need people have for belonging and for interaction. If you can offer that opportunity, you may be able to position yourself as a de facto leader – but beware the demands on time and energy that sustaining a tribe over the long term can entail.

- What could you achieve with the support of a critical mass of followers?
- Can you access these people easily? How could you attract them?
- Can you meet their needs for flourishing, interaction or growth?
- Do you have the time to facilitate and co-ordinate the interactions?

16 Build alliances

> 'Alone we can do so little; together we can do so much.'
> Helen Keller

> 'It is the long history of humankind (and animal kind, too): those who learned to collaborate and improvise most effectively have prevailed.' Charles Darwin

> 'I never trust a man unless I've got his pecker in my pocket.'
> President Lyndon B. Johnson

> 'If you do not seek out allies and helpers, then you will be isolated and weak.' Sun Tzu

> 'The forces of a powerful ally can be useful and good to those who have recourse to them… but are perilous to those who become dependent on them.' Niccolò Machiavelli

For all that you can achieve on your own, the chances are that you will achieve even more if you can collaborate with others. Effective politicians the world over have discovered that, however dogmatic their public rhetoric may be, achievement depends upon the ability to cut a deal, often directly with the 'enemy', and that compromise and collaboration are the only way to ensure results.

Alliances in business are often pragmatic; they exist solely to boost your chances of achieving your aims. They can be as formal or informal as you like; many of the more effective are between colleagues, and are short term, disbanded as soon as the mutual objective has been achieved. Indeed, retaining freedom of action is an important part of alliance building. These are not partnerships or coalitions. You don't want to find yourself tethered to an ally beyond the point at which the alliance stops bearing fruit.

At an individual level, alliances are simply a tool to help get things done. Working with colleagues within or across departments helps ensure that crucial decisions are made in your favour, budgets are protected and that key information is made available to you early.

At an organizational level, collaboration with competitors can achieve transformational economies of scale and genuine innovation.

The expert influencer needs to be adept at all three phases of alliance building, which are:

1. recognizing the opportunity for an alliance
2. identifying likely allies
3. facilitating the process from formation through execution to dissolution.

'Many hands make light work', as the saying goes, and an effective influencer will make it a priority to ensure that she can count on the right support when it is most needed.

MAKE ALLIANCES WITH COLLEAGUES

Do you struggle to get your voice heard in meetings? Do key decisions seem to go your way depressingly rarely? If so, perhaps you need to pay more attention to alliance building. Having a great idea or feeling strongly about something is simply not enough to ensure that your point of view will prevail. In order to get things done, you need to take account of the electoral arithmetic in your team, office or business. You need your view to be endorsed by the majority, or at least a majority of key players. And you garner support for your ideas not through silver-tongued rhetoric on the day or at a meeting, which will leave too much to chance, but through the prior accumulation of 'votes in the bank'.

Say you favour a change of supplier to your business. The decision will be taken at a monthly meeting at which five heads of department sit down and discuss matters of concern. You methodically prepare a business case, perhaps circulate it by email in advance, and then are surprised and hurt at the lack of buy-in on the day and failure to secure your preferred outcome.

The failure shouldn't come as a surprise. Most likely, no one read the email and, in the meeting, everyone feels blindsided.

Compare the genuine influencer's approach. She will 'take soundings' with the other four decision-makers before the key meeting has even been scheduled. She will float her idea casually, attaching no great importance to it, and test the response. Say one individual seems implacably opposed; another genuinely enthusiastic; the other two harder to read. She will concentrate her efforts on the two 'undecideds', exactly as a political party would focus its resources on marginal seats at election time. When one of those undecideds is persuaded, that's the time to put the item on the meeting agenda. Once you already have a majority on your side, the decision is in the bag before the meeting has begun.

MAKE ALLIANCES WITH COMPETITORS

The same approach can work between and among organizations, even if they are competitors. 'Sleeping with the enemy', far from compromising your organization's position, can actually bolster it. Again, it comes down to numbers, to critical mass. Discover a common goal, build a 'coalition of the willing' to help achieve the goal through collaboration rather than competition, and you have a very powerful model, particularly if you sit at the centre of it as creator or co-ordinator.

In the motor industry, for example, informal alliances between competitors are now commonplace. BMW and Toyota and General Motors and PSA Peugeot Citroën have alliances in place to co-develop fuel-saving technologies. The pooling of resources makes possible a level of investment that would be impossible without collaboration. Likewise, in the arts world, co-productions between apparently rival theatres and performing arts companies are now commonplace for similar reasons of economies of scale.

In your own sector, it may be that collaboration through informal alliances with your competitors may give your organization more clout or save it money. To protect your market position, however, it is best to select allies who are complementary rather than direct competitors. Perhaps you offer different services to the same market, or the same service to different markets.

Make sure that you take a key role in the unfolding alliance – become the 'point person' who initiates the arrangement and nurtures it. By doing so, you will likely access insight and privileged information that will make you an industry insider, a 'player', and your level of influence will grow exponentially.

FOSTER UNLIKELY ALLIANCES

Sometimes, reaching out to form an alliance with an unexpected partner can create spectacular results. Starbucks and PepsiCo might have seemed unlikely bedfellows, but the former's product development skill and the latter's formidable distribution network combined to create a whole new bottled-drinks sector, as anyone who fills their supermarket trolley with bottled Frappucino will know.

Seventies rock god Robert Plant and bluegrass musician Alison Krauss would not, on the face of it, appeal to the same sort of audience. Yet their 2007 collaboration *Raising Sand* became a platinum-selling mega-smash, winning both artists a completely new audience.

So make a point of tuning in not only to your own market, niche or sector, but also to complementary or even completely unconnected ones. Buy magazines you wouldn't normally read. Attend networking events with a broader constituency than usual. Start conversations with people who work in apparently unrelated spaces. You never know where it might lead…

What, then, are the keys to effective alliance building? First, begin with a specific objective in mind. What exactly do you want to achieve? Then draw up a list of possible collaborators, those who might be able to help you achieve your aim. Be careful to look beyond the usual suspects; perhaps support can come from unlikely quarters. Then try to be specific about the nature of support you are looking for; is it visible, flag-waving endorsement you are after or merely an agreement not to oppose?

Then begin to build your alliance, one bilateral conversation at a time. These conversations will need to focus on what's in it for your potential ally if they agree to collaborate. Sometimes, the goal itself is so palpably in their self-interest that their buy-in comes quickly; at other times, a trade-off may be necessary. In return for their support this time, can they bank on yours at some point in the future?

- What do you have to trade? Alliance building requires reciprocity, so if you ask for help, be sure to know how you can also give it.
- Whose help might you conceivably need 12 months from now?
- Consider your least likely ally. What opportunities would open up if you converted them?

17 Help others: go first

> 'Giving people self-confidence is by far the most important thing that I can do. Because then they will act.' Jack Welch

> 'It's that wonderful old-fashioned idea that others come first and you come second. This was the whole ethic by which I was brought up. Others matter more than you do, so "Don't fuss, dear; get on with it."' Audrey Hepburn

> 'I always tell my kids to cut a sandwich in half right when you get it, and the first thought you should have is somebody else. You only ever need half a burger.' Louis C.K.

> 'If you do a good job for others, you heal yourself at the same time, because a dose of joy is a spiritual cure.' Dietrich Bonhoeffer

> 'My piece of bread only belongs to me when I know that everyone else has a share, and that no one starves while I eat.' Leo Tolstoy

Most of what we want to achieve in life can be secured only with the co-operation – or at least consent – of other people. Therefore, the ability to influence others to help us or work with us becomes a critical life skill. The question is, how do we do it?

At one end of the spectrum is coercion, where we use status or hierarchical power to insist on other people's compliance. But, unless you happen to be the head of a totalitarian state or a commander in the armed forces, this is unlikely to be a practicable tactic for most people in everyday life. Instead, we are more likely to get people to do our bidding through subtler approaches, and, after enticement, which we have already considered, eliciting a sense of obligation can be helpful. We feel obliged to help those who have at some time or other helped us; the principle of reciprocity is very powerful in human relations. So we will stay late to help out a colleague who did the same for us a few weeks back. We will support the proposal of a colleague who put in a good word for us at promotion time.

Unsophisticated influencers will attempt to use the power of persuasion to get other people to do their bidding. Do this, they implore, simply because I am asking you to. But this approach is akin to cashing a cheque on an empty bank account: you have no credit to work with. We probably all have acquaintances who get in touch only when they want something, and whom we are rarely disposed to help.

By contrast, more savvy operators actively seek out opportunities to help other people. They go out of their way to offer assistance before it is asked for. I am not suggesting that this is done for any ulterior motive: helping others in and of itself seems a decent thing to do. But it is undeniable that, when we need the help of another person, he or she is more disposed to go along with the request if we already have in place a track record of being helpful to them.

Goodwill takes time to develop. Waste no opportunity to build up credit with other people, as you never know when you will need to cash that cheque.

RECOMMEND OTHERS

The personal referral is the most powerful endorsement of our skill or ability. If you are willing to put your own judgement on the line and recommend the services of someone, your view generally carries more weight than any number of Google ads or PR puffery. It's incredibly flattering to hear that a potential client has got in touch with us 'because X or Y recommended you'. And yet we don't use this simple tactic anything like enough. Perhaps because we are so bound up with our own affairs, we miss the multiple opportunities for other people that our networks and contacts throw up every day.

Be on the lookout for opportunities for others. Provide LinkedIn references for people before they ask for them. Make it your business to help other people grow theirs. It is likely to take you very little time and cost you nothing, but the goodwill you establish will be enormous.

BE A FRIEND INDEED TO THOSE IN NEED

How attuned are you to the stresses and strains of other people's lives – particularly those you work with? Because of the way we compartmentalize ourselves, it is often possible to work closely with someone for years and know next to nothing about their real state of mind. Hence the oft-heard refrain when illness – or worse – afflicts a co-worker: 'I had no idea anything was wrong.'

I am not suggesting that you pry into people's private lives, or become the office agony aunt or uncle. However, being emotionally intelligent enough to pick up when someone's spirits are flagging or when they seem unusually distracted shouldn't be beyond us. A supportive word, a friendly ear, a sense that you are happy to be a non-judgemental sounding board if required can be enormously comforting.

Linda, a senior manager in the financial services sector, makes a telling observation:

'I think, generally, women are better at this than men. I think some men are scared that if they "cross the line" and start to initiate conversations about people's wider lives, they are opening themselves up to misinterpretation or expectations beyond their pay grade. But I do spend time each week listening to what's going on in my team's lives. People are not automatons – real life will always intrude. And, while I don't in any sense presume to offer solutions, I can certainly offer support and sometimes that is all that matters.'

APPRECIATE GOOD WORK

Performance management is one of those dread phrases that deadens the soul: often it is used as a way of justifying criticism or preparing for a 'hard' conversation. In managing others, we are on the constant lookout for their deficiencies and flaws; the good stuff often gets missed. Research, however, has shown that praise and positive reinforcement are some of the most effective 'performance management' tools at our disposal.

We need to look consciously for opportunities to recognize effort, attitude and achievement. A quiet word, a one-line email or a handwritten note acknowledging good performance can be more motivating than a pay rise. Why don't we do it more?

It's true that it can be overdone, and insincerity in praise giving is probably worse than saying nothing at all. But the fact remains that most people, in work, relationships and life in general would admit to feeling underappreciated. You have multiple opportunities every day to make a difference to that perception.

Putting it all together

Helping people, going first in attempting to build credit in relationships, facilitates influence on several levels. Robert Cialdini, in his 1984 book *Influence: The Psychology of Persuasion*, noted liking and reciprocity as powerful forces in holding sway over others. Being proactive in seeking opportunities to help and support others will clearly do our chances of being liked by them no harm at all. And in the longer term, provided we are not seen to have been motivated entirely by self-interest, others will be keen to reciprocate by pledging their time, effort and energy to our cause when we need them.

Note: this is a long-term investment strategy, not a quick fix. You will be kidding no one if some unusually positive feedback from you one week is followed by a request to work late the next!

- When was the last time you gave someone some unsolicited, positive feedback?
- Which of your contacts could most benefit from a referral from you right now?
- When did you last take the time to listen to a co-worker or friend discuss non-work-related issues?

18 Listen

> 'In some South Pacific cultures, a speaker holds a conch shell as a symbol of temporary position of authority. Leaders must understand who holds the conch — that is, who should be listened to and when.' **Max De Pree**

> 'Silence is a source of great strength.' **Lao Tzu**

> 'We should never pretend to know what we don't know, we should not feel ashamed to ask and learn from people below, and we should listen carefully to the views of the cadres at the lowest levels. Be a pupil before you become a teacher; learn from the cadres at the lower levels before you issue orders.' **Mao Tse-tung**

> 'Any problem, big or small, within a family, always seems to start with bad communication. Someone isn't listening.' **Emma Thompson**

> 'Leadership to me means duty, honor, country. It means character, and it means listening from time to time.' **George W. Bush**

I don't know about you, but I must have missed listening class at school. I remember the maths and the spelling and the long jump, but help with the most important life skill of all? Zilch.

Listening ought to make it on to the national curriculum because it is so imperfectly practised in adulthood. We may often give the *appearance* of listening, but in our head something else is happening. We're rehearsing our interruption. We're finding fault or flaw with the speaker. We're daydreaming about the great evening that lies ahead once we get out of the company of the idiot who's sitting opposite us opening and closing his mouth…

There's a reason we rarely commit to 'proper' listening: it's such damned hard work. Shutting off the myriad distractions in our own minds and attending completely to another person, noting all those incongruences between words and tone and body language… it's exhausting. It's much easier to operate instead on the basis of assumption, misinterpretation and plain old wrong-headedness, which, of course, is the natural habitat of the mediocre listener.

World-class influencers know differently. Listening was the skill many of the people interviewed for this book said they had to work on the most. They also said that it was worth the effort, because people can only be influenced once their positions are truly understood. Without that level of understanding, the influencer is always working on the basis of hope rather than expectation.

Great influencers seem to have an intuitive grasp of the ebb and flow of conversation: when to shut up, in other words, and when to proceed.

'It's the one thing I discovered late in my career that I wish I'd known about earlier,' says a retired executive. 'I always thought leadership was about having your view prevail, shouting the loudest, if you like. But really listening to other people is not only occasionally enlightening, it's also intensely practical. You have to carry people with you, and if they have reservations, better you know about them sooner rather than later. If you'd listened, you could have nipped in the bud the little misgivings that hardened into prejudices that later on derailed your best plans…'

GET THE INTROVERTS TALKING

In order to listen, other people must be talking, which sometimes means you have to invite their contributions. This can often be a difficult concept for extrovert types to understand. Used to giving their view without solicitation, enjoying nothing more than a bit of brainstorming, these characters are often oblivious to the fact that more introverted personalities wait to be invited to contribute. It's not standoffishness or lack of engagement; it's just different wiring. Unless you create an environment where less forceful types feel they can be heard, you will be missing out on the considered opinion of about half your colleagues.

Even when they are invited to contribute, the response from more introverted colleagues may not be immediately forthcoming. It may not be fluent. You will need to give these speakers time and space to express themselves. But there is likely to be a pay-off in getting the quieter types talking, as Tricia, a law firm partner, discovered.

'You get a completely different perspective from reflective types. They see things you might have missed because you were too busy talking. The introverts are always the more reliable witnesses in trial situations – they are often attuned to mood and subtext far better than more extrovert types. Internally, I try to encourage contributions from quieter colleagues and really pay attention to what they say, because it is sometimes a revelation.'

LISTEN WITH YOUR EYES

No communication-skills training course is complete without reference to the so-called Mehrabian Rule, based on the work of the social scientist Albert Mehrabian. Although the circumstances of his research are often misinterpreted, in the popular mind he was the first to establish the extraordinary importance of non-verbal aspects of communication. His magic numbers are 55/38/7: he posited that 7 per cent of the meaning of an interaction comes from the words themselves, 38 per cent from tone of voice, and a whopping 55 per cent from non-verbal means – that is, body language. While the figures themselves may be disputed, it is undeniable that, if we don't pay attention to tone of voice and body language, then, frankly, we are just not properly listening.

It's in the discrepancies between the words and their tone that much meaning is revealed. For example, the word 'fine' can mean complete acquiescence or anything but, depending on the inflection. How much attention do you pay to tone? In the pressure of the moment, do you take everything at face value and miss the reservations underneath? Police interrogators are trained to spot 'clusters' of body language: the rubbing of the neck, the touching of the nose – meaning nothing much when done separately – which together could be indicative of discomfort or unease.

Real listening doesn't just pay attention to the words. It involves an awareness of all the subtle communication signals emanating from across the table. And if there seems to be some incongruence, isn't it worth stopping to explore it? It is said that the subconscious 'leaks' through our body language: that it is possible to spot the difference between compliance and commitment through non-verbal cues. When you are influencing someone, it is worth knowing the difference. Commitment ensures that an action will be carried out. Mere compliance means that more persuasion is needed: conflict between the words and the body language can give you an early clue.

REFLECT AND SUMMARIZE

It is not enough just to listen; you need to give people evidence of your listening. And the easiest way to do that is to become adept at the use of playing people's words back to them:

- 'When you say that…'
- 'Tell me what you mean by…'
- 'So your main issues are…'

Demonstrating that you are really listening is one of the quickest ways to build trust, and the techniques of reflection and summarizing – not paraphrasing, which indicates at best imperfect listening – are critical to this.

It is said of the great negotiators that only when they understand the other side's position better than they do themselves do they begin to formulate their strategy. The same could be said of any personal interaction: people are only willing to be influenced once they feel they have been truly heard.

'It's almost as if you can see them sigh with relief,' says one experienced manager. 'If you can play back exactly what they told you, that's the moment when they give tacit permission for you to put across your view. That's when they are willing to be persuaded. But it's not until they are certain you've got it – that you understand what they really think or feel or fear.'

Putting it all together

In his landmark book *7 Habits of Highly Effective People*, first published in 1989, Stephen Covey talked about seeking first to understand, then to be understood. The order hasn't changed, it's just that people's preparedness to wait their turn before having their say seems to have diminished. Real listening is so rare that it almost confers on the expert practitioner a mystical quality. Listening is the ultimate courtesy and the ultimate seduction. Maybe it deserves its place alongside quadratic equations on the school syllabus?

- Who are the introverts in your life? When did you last invite them to contribute to discussion? When did you give them the time to express themselves at their own pace in their own way?
- How closely do you attend to the body language and tone of voice of people you communicate with? Do you notice inconsistencies or contradictions?
- When did you last play back someone's words to them? How closely can you recollect the exact words in the last meaningful conversation you had?

19 Speak their language

> **❝** '*I work really hard at trying to see the big picture and not getting stuck in ego. I believe we're all put on this planet for a purpose, and we all have a different purpose... When you connect with that love and that compassion, that's when everything unfolds.*' Ellen DeGeneres

> **❝** '*In order to properly understand the big picture, everyone should fear becoming mentally clouded and obsessed with one small section of truth.*' Xun Zi

> **❝** '*It is the obvious which is so difficult to see most of the time. People say "It's as plain as the nose on your face." But how much of the nose on your face can you see, unless someone holds a mirror up to you?*' Isaac Asimov, I, Robot

> **❝** '*If there is any one secret of success, it lies in the ability to get the other person's point of view and see things from that person's angle as well as from your own.*' Henry Ford

> **❝** '*You like potato and I like potahto*
> *You like tomato and I like tomahto*
> *Potato, potahto, tomato, tomahto.*
> *Let's call the whole thing off...*' George and Ira Gershwin

Kate had a problem. As Director of Marketing for a major retailer, she felt frustrated at the lack of buy-in she was getting at board level, particularly in the area of social media. She was a real enthusiast for new marketing channels and had begun to feel deflated that the board didn't seem to share her passion.

'They just don't seem to get it,' she told me one day. 'Maybe it's a generational thing – they're mostly 50-something guys who think they're being tech-savvy by showing up in the office with an iPad. But when I gave a presentation a couple of weeks ago showing how our non-existent social media strategy was hurting us, I could see them glazing over and thinking about the evening's restaurant reservation.'

I asked her to outline the bare bones of her presentation. She said she had based it around the case study of a small, independent food and drink manufacturer that had leveraged social media and increased turnover by 110 per cent in just over a year. She had gone on to outline the various channels that the company could utilize – Twitter, Facebook and so on – and finished with a carefully costed proposal for increased spend on social marketing in the next financial year.

Even as she was giving me this outline, Kate began to see the flaws in the way she had gone about the presentation:

- Unrelated case study (food and beverage producer with £3 million turnover vs. global retailer with £6 billion turnover)
- Telling them what they already knew (pale and male they may have been, but the board didn't need an idiot's guide to social media; they mostly had teenage kids)
- Costs before benefits (was she really expecting the CFO to open his chequebook to find the additional £300,000 she was asking for when he'd spent the meeting telling all departments to cut their budgets by an additional 5 per cent?).

I asked what the board tended to spend its time talking about. Kate was not a board member, but she had attended enough meetings to be able to answer immediately.

'Risk and compliance,' she said. The light bulb went on immediately, and the next presentation began to form.

SEE THE BIGGER PICTURE

Naturally, we don't like to think of our own issues and concerns as irrelevant. We spend a lot of time mulling them over, and they can start to assume immense proportions. This is a huge bear trap for the unwary influencer: to avoid it, get a sense of perspective before using your own yardstick to measure a problem.

Kate had made her board presentation from her own perspective: social media was the buzz in the marketing world, and she attempted to persuade by pulling the innovation and peer-pressure levers: come on guys, this stuff is really exciting, let's not be late getting on the bus!

The board's concerns were entirely different: risk management was front and centre of their agenda. There were no guarantees, of course, but perhaps Kate would have been more influential if she had framed her entire message in terms of the reputational damage that could be inflicted on the business if social media channels were not proactively managed. A more persuasive, and certainly better aligned, argument might have been one around the nature of the threat rather than the size of the opportunity.

Particularly when influencing up, we need to be sure we have complete clarity about the frame of reference of the person we are trying to influence. If it differs from our own, it is our approach that will need flexing, not that of the more senior stakeholder.

ALIGN YOUR METRICS

Data overwhelms us. We have more tools and metrics at our fingertips than could possibly have been conceived a mere half-decade ago. This data avalanche can produce one of two dangerous reactions, neither of which is effective in our attempts to influence.

Some people become data-avoiders. The sight of an Excel spreadsheet brings them out in a rash. Too much, they cry, too much. Their data aversion leaves them open to easy rebuttal: their arguments are based on false premises and assumptions, or they overestimate the power of their charm and charisma to persuade.

Then there are the data-obsessives. They get IT to design bespoke metrics and charts. They slice and dice in hitherto unimagined ways. They definitely have the data – it's just that it doesn't correspond with anyone else's. There is no point in bringing in three pages of website data usage if all that matters to your boss is bounce rate.

There is no doubt that data can be useful in trying to influence a decision; it is just worth while checking which data is most relevant to your audience before bamboozling them with figures.

REACH OUT

It's a rare organization of any size that doesn't encounter the problems associated with silo mentality. There must be something deep in the human psyche that impels us to find our tribe, huddle together and ward off imagined invaders. What may have proved a necessary form of defence in Neanderthal times is actually the source of most misunderstanding and stalemate in organizations.

If you really want to break down the walls the better to understand another team's agenda – so that in future you can influence them far more effectively – why not reach out to them? Invite them to be part of your team's planning sessions. Ask for their advice on your strategy. Show some basic curiosity about them.

'You have to be willing to go first,' says Dan, who works in a division of a consultancy firm. 'Inertia is very prevalent in organizations, and so are turf wars and siege mentality. Waiting for change is often fruitless; you have to make it happen. When I suggested to one of the other teams that they might like to join forces and come with us on our away day, a few people thought I was mad. But we cleared up more misunderstandings that day than we would have achieved any other way – and we found out that what we thought was obstruction on their part was actually prudent risk management. It's not perfect now, but at least we know where each other is coming from…'

Until you know your target's frame of reference, it is very difficult to implement a strategy that will influence them. You will be like a salesman in a strange town who doesn't speak the local language. No matter how useful your product or service, you won't close many sales if you are perpetually unintelligible or allow your benefits and features to be lost in translation.

- In a situation where you want to exert influence, how well do you understand the strategic imperatives of the other side?
- Do you use data to support your case? Do your metrics align with those you are trying to persuade?
- Who could you reach out to? Who do you need to understand better?

20 Introduce people

Anthony – who works for one of the UK's 'Big Four' accountants – was one of those people whose name kept cropping up in other conversations. People in banking would mention his name. People in industry would mention his name. It was when I was having a chat with someone who runs a children's charity, and his name was called out again, that I thought I had better try to meet him.

For someone who seemed so influential, he was remarkably easy to reach. He answered his own phone and readily agreed to a coffee. When we met, I mentioned the fact that his name seemed widely known.

'I have only ever had one marketing strategy,' he said simply. 'I don't give talks and I don't write articles. I just introduce people.'

People can be incredibly protective of their networks. On LinkedIn, people have an option to conceal who they know, and they use it. In certain firms, senior people never let their juniors meet their clients. There is a scarcity mentality at work: if I share my contacts, my network will become diluted. 'I will keep my contacts to myself, so they are mine, all mine!'

Anthony's view was different:

'Number one, it generates the best return on investment I know. Putting people in touch with one other takes little time and effort, yet people are incredibly grateful if it turns out to be a worthwhile relationship. The other thing is that it confers authority and status on me: I appear to be a connector, someone who knows people. Actually, I can think of other colleagues who have far more diverse networks than me, but they don't have this image because they don't share who they know. And finally, of course, there is the wonderful rule of reciprocation. Once I make an introduction that turns out to be pretty useful, the beneficiary is usefully minded to try to return the favour."

A week or so after our interview, the phone rang and it was Anthony.

'I met an entrepreneur the other night at an award do, one of these "most influential under 30" types. Great guy. I talked about your book to him and said I'd put the two of you in touch…'

LOOK FOR A WIN–WIN

This is not a technique to be used without thought. Making a bad introduction – wasting two people's time – is likely to backfire on you spectacularly. The key is to bring two people together for their mutual benefit. This is harder to achieve than you may at first think.

In most business relationships, there is a buyer and a seller. The buyer, most of the time, is in a superior position, and this can make for an uncomfortable first meeting of strangers. The seller doesn't want to overtly sell; the buyer doesn't want to feel compelled to buy. Far better to find a meeting of equals – and the common ground may not be business at all.

Here is Anthony again:

'The best introductions are the ones done on the basis of a mutual interest: people who support the same teams, who want to get involved in similar sorts of charitable work, that sort of thing. Unless a contact of mine made a very specific request for a recommendation – "I'm looking for an IP lawyer" – I wouldn't tend to bring people together on a buyer/seller basis.'

The biggest win–win, then, is often the prospect of meeting someone where there is some common ground rather than the sense of an immediate sale. The challenge is remembering this information, so it is useful to find a means of recording people's interests to make the process of constructive introductions even easier.

SHARE CONTACTS ONLINE AND THROUGH SOCIAL MEDIA

Anthony is a great believer in the face-to-face meet-up. Of course, this carries with it some risk: you may not find the common ground you were after and you've wasted a lunchtime.

This is where introductions via social networks can be very effective. The strategy here can be one to one again – you drop an email to someone specific, suggesting they check out your contact's blog or website – or it can be broader. A recommendation online – taking the form of a retweet, for example, or a post on LinkedIn – can give your contact exposure to the whole of your network very quickly. The rule of reciprocity kicks in here as well, as Carmen who is a freelance designer noticed:

'I tweeted about a new show opening in a local gallery because I genuinely love this artist and I knew my friends would be interested. It then got picked up by the artist himself, who retweeted to all his followers, and loads of conversations got started. This is the kind of thing that happens on Twitter – it's very circular. So I just wanted to let my friends know about this show, then the guy himself unleashes all of his contacts to me. All through 140 characters!'

MAKE THE MOST OF THE RULE OF RECIPROCITY

Your motivation in making the introduction is, of course benign: you have been impressed by the individuals concerned and are keen to assist them in the building up of their network. There is, though, the possibility that you will gain from the action just as much as the people you have introduced – they will feel obliged to return the favour.

The final word is from matchmaker extraordinaire, Anthony:

'Once I have made the introduction I will stand back a bit; the last thing the two people want is me turning up and sitting like an idiot in between them. I will speak to them both separately, though, and find out how things went. Eventually, if I'm organizing a social event or a round table, I will bring all three of us together, and that's usually the point at which there's a click. "Oh yes, Antony, it's you we have to thank for this hugely constructive new friendship," and that's when I'll usually add to my own network too, by reciprocation. And if it's not forthcoming, I will sometimes just say, "It would be good if you could put me in touch with someone in the XX industry." And I'll know this is a connection they can make, and because I went first, they will by and large do what they can to facilitate that introduction.'

Throughout this book, it's the abundance mentality that seems to win out over scarcity, and never is that more true than in the case of sharing your contacts and introducing people to each other. Unless you are in direct competition with the people you are making introductions to, the chances are your relationships will be strengthened, not weakened, by this approach.

- Which people in your network might benefit from meeting one other? What is the link or common ground?
- Who have you recommended online? Can you draw attention to a contact's website?
- After making an introduction, how can you, tactfully, 'keep some skin in the game'? Would you ever ask directly for a referral?

21 Go analogue

> '*I have to be seen to be believed.*' attr. Queen Elizabeth II

> '*I don't believe in email. I'm an old-fashioned girl. I prefer calling and hanging up.*' Sarah Jessica Parker

> '*The least-crowded channel for meeting high-profile bloggers is in person. Email is the most difficult, the most crowded… I'm a top 1,000 blogger, not a top 100 blogger, and I get hundreds of pitches by email every week. Most of them I don't even see because my assistant declines them.*' Timothy Ferriss

> '*For people who have been raised on text-based interactions, just speaking on the telephone can be high bandwidth to the point of anxiety.*' Daniel H. Wilson

> '*[I]nnovation comes from people meeting up in the hallways or calling each other at 10.30 at night with a new idea, or because they realized something that shoots holes in how we've been thinking about a problem.*' Steve Jobs

Most of us are groaning under the weight of information overload. In the minute or so it takes you to read this page, some 200 million emails will be sent, 6 million Facebook pages viewed and 100,000 tweets launched upon the world.

If, for some unfathomable reason, you wanted to watch all the video crossing the Internet in just one second, it would take around five years of your life. That's days and nights. It's worse the younger you are: US teenagers send, on average, over 3,000 SMS messages a month. Thts lots of txt lol.

It's too much 'stuff'. No wonder we're feeling stressed. In fact, a recent Loughborough University study showed a direct link between stress levels and email: office workers showed raised cortisol levels and increased blood pressure and heart rate when they were sending and receiving emails.

The surfeit of information, and the increasingly impersonal and automated nature of our daily interactions, presents a real opportunity for the influencer. Just as more and more people are immersing more of themselves in digital and online methods of communication, the old-fashioned, more personal, approaches are acquiring real scarcity value. And if one of the keys to being influential is an ability to stand out from the crowd, particularly in the way one interacts with and persuades other people, then mastering the analogue approach can produce powerful results.

'Analogue' means any form of communication that takes people out of the virtual world and reminds them that there is a real one! It is anything that is spontaneous, takes some effort and adds a personal touch. The approaches that follow may be time consuming but they stand a real chance of making the message and thus the messenger memorable. Precisely because they take effort, they are likely to be appreciated, often disproportionately so, and enhance the influencer's reputation.

REMEMBER HANDWRITING

How often do we handwrite anything these days? We write cheques (soon to be defunct). We scribble shopping lists (now less necessary with the increase in online grocery shopping). We make notes in meetings (in the absence of tablets). It has become unusual to see and recognize our own handwriting, let alone other people's. That is exactly why Simon, a divisional executive at a large pharmaceutical company, makes a habit of writing personal thank-you notes to members of his staff.

'I think we need to fight hard to retain the personal touch in large organizations. It can all become too inhuman with the use of all the IT now. So if someone goes the extra mile – maybe stays late to finish a project, or comes in on their day off to help us get something out – I will always drop them a few lines of thanks in a card. I could do the same in an email, of course, but it just wouldn't have the same impact. People have told me they take the cards home and show them to their families. It makes them feel good about themselves. It's a small outlay of effort on my part, but because it does show some effort and it is personal, it seems to matter. Voicing your appreciation of others is a really underrated management tool in terms of the goodwill it generates – people are far more willing to put themselves out for you if they know it will not go unnoticed or taken for granted.'

For the same reason, we may want to reconsider our approach to the sending of Christmas cards. There has been a massive trend away from sending these in favour of e-cards and charitable donations in recent years. We believe that demonstrating our environmental credentials and our charitable works is more important than a few scrawled words on a piece of paper. The downside is that a valuable means of personal connection is lost. Perhaps it should be a both/and rather than either/or – make your donations, but send a few cards, too. The personal message may generate goodwill that outlasts the festive season.

PICK UP THE PHONE

Many of us will be able to think of examples of work colleagues – sitting metres away from each other – who communicate with each other via email rather than talk. Email is the default communication medium of our times. It has its limitations, though, as private equity specialist David explains:

'We waste so much time through email. It is one-way communication, it clogs up the other person's inbox and it just destroys productivity. I tell all my people to make more use of the phone. It is two way, you can get decisions made quickly, and you also form much more of a personal bond. People often hide behind email, particularly if they are dealing with different parts of the world, but nine times out of ten you can achieve what you want far more quickly over the phone than by email.'

Of course, the phone is a far riskier form of communication. The other person may not welcome the intrusion, or may say something you don't like or were not expecting. Yet, in hearing and responding to the other person's tone of voice, you can avoid so many of the misunderstandings that often follow when you rashly hit 'send'.

GET OUT MORE

It's over 30 years since Tom Peters and Bob Waterman coined the term MBWA – managing by wandering around – in their book *In Search of Excellence.* Since then, despite the prevalence of open-plan offices, we seem to have become ever more closely chained to our desks. The computer screen exerts its tyrannical hold, whatever line of work we're in. It's incredibly difficult to influence from a permanently seated, eye-contact-avoidant position, however.

Influencers break away from their desk on a regular basis, and make a point of accidentally-on-purpose bumping into colleagues. 'How's things with you?' they'll ask. 'What are you working on?' Through such low-key, regular, face-to-face interactions are visibility raised, intelligence gathered and rapport established. The higher you are in the hierarchy, the greater the need for this kind of interaction. Queen Elizabeth II, defending her public walkabouts from the paranoia of her security advisers, is said to have declared that the monarch had to be 'seen to be believed'. The same is true of executives and managers – influencers.

'If people don't see me regularly in the flesh,' one CEO told me, 'they start mythologizing. I end up in the corporate consciousness looking like Mr Burns from *The Simpsons*. If they see me and we have a bit of inane chat, they realize I'm just a normal guy. Putting on weight, struggling to get time with the kids, not getting any younger. That stuff matters – the personal connection, the face time.'

Putting it all together

It's a matter of balance, of course. You can't go around writing notes to or shaking the hands of hundreds of colleagues – you might come across as a little too much like a career politician for your own good. But for those you are keenest to influence, the handful of people whose buy-in you are desperate to acquire, the sincere use of these old-fashioned techniques can make a difference.

If revenge is a dish best served cold, then appreciation, gratitude and curiosity about others' lives are best served warm. And for all their power, information technology and social media cannot (yet!) communicate human warmth, which is why the phone, the pen and the face-to-face meeting retain such power and should be used rather more frequently than they are.

- Can you use the phone more?
- Would people know your handwriting if they saw it?
- Do you wander around?

Part 3

What you do: influence through productivity

22 Give great value: over-deliver

> 'I value the friend who for me finds time on his calendar, but I cherish the friend who for me does not consult his calendar.'
> **Robert Brault**

> 'Price is what you pay. Value is what you get.' Warren Buffett

> 'The habit of doing more than is necessary can only be earned through practice.' Seth Godin

> 'The first step in exceeding your customers' expectations is to know those expectations.' Roy H. Williams

> 'Do what you do so well that they will want to see it again and bring their friends.' Walt Disney

I once booked a day tour of the Australian rainforest. The guide was extremely knowledgeable and we spent the day admiring all manner of flora and fauna. We'd been told to bring our own provisions, so lunch was a makeshift affair by the edge of a waterfall. By mid-afternoon, after several hours in the heat, most of our party were flagging. At exactly this moment, the guide brought us to a forest clearing, sat us down and, unannounced, handed around glasses of the freshest, coldest mango juice and watermelon juice imaginable, which we drank to the sound of parrots and kookaburras squawking in the canopy above.

In a hotel in Asia, I was asked on arrival which newspaper I wanted delivered to the room in the morning. I mentioned two titles, but it was clear neither was available. The receptionist offered profuse apologies, and I happily settled on a third more readily available option. Imagine the impression when, next morning, I found hanging on the doorknob not just the newspaper we had agreed on, but both of my initial requests, photocopied and meticulously bound.

My family has a range of takeaway restaurants to choose from near where we live. We always default to the same one, however. The reason is the little selection of chutneys and appetizers that come at no charge with the order, which for my kids tends to be the best part of the meal.

The juice, the newspaper and the chutneys: in actual cost terms to the supplier, relative to the price of the tour, the room and the meal, they are negligible, but in terms of perceived value to me they are enormous.

We are so accustomed to feeling ripped off or exploited that when one of those rare moments comes along when it feels as if we are getting real additional value – something for nothing – it makes an extraordinary impression.

Differentiation is one of the keys to influence. Being a person known to offer great value, who exceeds expectations, will certainly differentiate you from the majority of your peers, colleagues and competitors.

ESTABLISH THEIR MOST VALUED CURRENCY

In the rainforest, the guide could have shown me any number of different bird species that hot and humid afternoon. He could have gone into overdrive about the threat to local fauna that the gradual encroachment of human beings provides. None of this would have impressed me at the time. My need was not for more knowledge; it was for liquid refreshment.

In order to over-deliver, we must understand what our stakeholders' 'most valued currency' (MVC) is. Until we really understand what matters to them, our efforts at over-delivering may end up as wasted effort.

MVCs vary enormously. In some situations it will be time, in others quality. Some people will see value in not having to micromanage you, others in the fact that you ask how their weekend went. Remember, true value, like beauty, rests in the eye of the beholder.

This tactic is of particular relevance when you are trying to influence up. One of the common responses when we asked people how their junior staff could gain influence was 'Understand what matters to me and deliver it.'

One manager commented:

'I think new hires begin to gain influence when they begin to understand that I'm not after bland acceptance. I actually want to hear their point of view. So it's when I see younger members of the team questioning something or offering a counter-proposal that I really start to take them seriously.'

Of course, another manager may value the efficient execution of his instructions more than people challenging them. To over-deliver you need to establish the other person's MVC.

MAKE REALISTIC PROMISES

There are two parts to the value equation: what you deliver and what is expected. The old saw says that we should under-promise and over-deliver. I'm not sure about the first part. Consciously underselling your abilities, or setting the lowest possible quality threshold, is unlikely to win you a place at the top table.

More often, however, people fall into the opposite trap: talking up what is possible to the extent that disappointment is the inevitable result. Not all of this is the result of the 'bullsh*t tendency'. It is often the result of a simple desire to please – and it happens fairly often around timescales.

Consider the following example. A client asks you for an urgent piece of work to be delivered by Thursday – a timescale you know to be extremely challenging. Which of these responses sounds like you?

- A: 'Thursday? Got it. No problem, no problem at all.' Puts phone down and thinks: 'Oh no.'
- B: 'Thursday?' Sharp intake of breath and tut-tutting sound. 'I've got a lot on this week. To be honest, Thursday, no

that's, er, a real problem. No can do, I'm afraid. I'm absolutely snowed under.'

- C:'I can certainly get you something by Thursday. I'm
  busy this week, so I need to understand what you are
  looking for. Tell me a bit more about your own deadlines
  and I'll see what I can do.'

Are you the fall guy, the pessimist or the pragmatist?

We hear a lot about the need to 'manage expectations' – which
strikes me as a rather sinister phrase. Surely the truth is that
we just need to be simultaneously completely honest and
completely helpful: not being so keen to please that we set
ourselves up for a fall, nor so introspective that we fail to see
the possibilities for offering value when they present themselves.

KEEP REMINDING THEM OF YOUR VALUE

Get a reputation for offering great value, and the chances are you
will win friends, clients and supporters and enjoy some success.
Over time, however, your reputation for value might begin to
erode. People expect it of you. It's the norm – not news any more.

One of our clients at a large professional firm wanted to
demonstrate value to its clients by offering to run training
sessions at the client's offices whenever there was a new move
in the market, so they could be seen to be educating the client
and sharing their formidable market knowledge. The client loved
these events – they took place three or four times a year, and
the room would be packed with the client's staff wanting to be
updated on market movements for free.

The firm was surprised then to be told one day that the client
was reviewing its advisers and that the firm would have to repitch
for the account. The driver, the firm was told, was entirely financial.

'Our new FD is determined to get added value from our
suppliers because he thinks firms like yours charge too much and
deliver too little.'

The firm went away and prepared for the pitch by calculating
the cost of the training sessions they had put together over the
years, together with an approximation of the value the client's

team had derived from them. The total figure, which they presented in their pitch, nearly equated to the fees the firm had charged.

'You mean we're net beneficiaries from your service?' asked the incredulous FD. 'Then why on earth didn't you say so?'

From that point on, the firm made a point of sending its clients a quarterly statement of their 'value added' activity, making sure that the lengths it went to to provide value to the client were neither overlooked nor taken for granted.

It's important that a track record of over-delivery is recognized. Perhaps you could keep a record of when you have gone the extra mile to refer to at appraisal time, or ask for a recommendation on LinkedIn that makes specific reference to your timekeeping, your eye for detail or the fact that you were happy to take a call at 3 a.m. on a Sunday morning.

Putting it all together

Most of us try to do what is asked of us. We are given an instruction, and we attempt to fulfil it to the best of our ability. Unfortunately, this is not a strategy likely to win influence or acquire differentiation. By contrast, a minority of people will take an instruction as a starting point and work out ways in which they can surpass expectations and delight jaded palates. An even smaller minority don't even wait for the instruction: for them, adding value is all about surprise and proactivity – giving assistance where it wasn't necessarily expected or even sought.

What's your approach to giving value? Do you give just enough – or do you take the view that 'the more the merrier'?

- How could you exceed someone's expectations? What would they most value?
- How often do you concede that something you promised cannot be delivered?
- When did you last remind your boss/client/significant other of the value you provide?

23 Make a wider contribution

> 'Life is not accumulation, it is about contribution.' Stephen Covey

> 'It is the ultimate luxury to combine passion and contribution. It's also a very clear path to happiness.' Sheryl Sandberg

> 'Legacy is not what's left tomorrow when you're gone. It's what you give, create, impact and contribute today while you're here that then happens to live on.' Rasheed Ogunlaru

> 'We are not here merely to make a living. We are here to enrich the world.' Woodrow Wilson

> 'It is high time that the ideal of success should be replaced by the ideal of service.' Albert Einstein

What sort of contribution do you make? You probably juggle a series of roles – worker, parent, relationship partner – that carry with them a set of pre-ordained responsibilities. And there's nothing wrong with seeing the carrying out of those responsibilities to the best of your ability as your main way of making a contribution.

Somehow, though, the influential manage to extend the field of play beyond their allocated titles and job description. Their contribution is felt in diverse and unexpected areas. They are not afraid to dip a toe in new and untested water, just to see what sort of ripple they might make.

In turn, this sense of a 'wider contribution' is often seen as a marker of potential leadership, and in some cases a selection criterion for top jobs. Beyond the technical ability, beyond the narrow field of your expertise, what *more* can you offer us, interview panels increasingly ask.

Beyond the immediate requirements of your role, a vast hinterland exists where it is possible to make a substantial impact. There's the rest of your organization, for a start; then the community in which you spend most of your time; and the whole wide world beyond that.

Why bother? Isn't the day job challenging and time-consuming enough? An executive headhunter explained why it might be worth the effort:

'Firms are looking for evidence of "outside the box" thinking. If you've been stuck in your silo for ten years, you are not likely to have the breadth of vision that an organization would be looking for from its senior team. If you've deliberately sought out new environments, you may have developed new skills and rubbed shoulders with different people, so you are seen as more marketable. Internally, too, it's the people who try to make a difference over and above their contractual obligations that get identified as ones to watch.'

You may not feel the need to get out more – but unfortunately just doing the day job barely covers the price of entry to influence these days. To be noticed, you need to show up in different worlds.

MAKE A WIDER CONTRIBUTION IN YOUR ORGANIZATION

'Contribution' possibly needs a little more explanation. It is emphatically not self-serving, so any exercise that is undertaken for the sole purpose of gaining you more profile or exposure does not count, and is likely to do more harm than good. The sort of contribution that matters is where you dedicate time and energy to helping your organization achieve its strategic ends rather than your narrow, tactical ones. It is 'showing willing'; it is engaging with bigger issues than those that directly affect you or your team.

There are always emails floating around asking for volunteers to join a steering group, or asking for views on a new product or location. Pitch up. Join the conversation. Put some time in.

Ed, a lawyer with a couple of years' post-qualification experience, did just that:

'The firm was having trouble retaining people and the management team was looking for ideas. So I put my hat in the ring and turned up at a couple of meetings and even attended a day long off-site. I have some strong views about the subject, which I tried to air sensitively. I was asked if I would help put together some options in a paper for the board, which I did even though it ended up being quite a big time commitment. I was interested in the subject, which helped, but it did definitely get me into the orbit of senior players. It was a big ask to engage in all this stuff after a day's work, but I'm glad I did.'

Anything that involves you with change and aligns you with wider strategy, that offers the chance to research the market and offer a view, could well be a good use of your time – even after hours on a wet Wednesday evening.

MAKE A WIDER CONTRIBUTION TO YOUR LOCAL COMMUNITY

Most organizations today take their corporate and social responsibility seriously, but sometimes there is a disconnect between well-meaning policy statements released by a head office on the other side of the world and the profile an organization has in its own community. Initiatives where an organization 'gets its hands dirty' in the local community can be beneficial in terms of public profile, but also give employees a chance to put their skills to a new and energizing use.

Many professional firms encourage 'pro bono' activities, where professional services are given free of charge to local charities. Helen, an accountant, got involved in a local programme assisting with numeracy among young adults in her local community.

'It was a great a scheme, a drop-in centre. The commitment was for a couple of hours a month for six months, and I got to meet some great people and build up some solid relationships. There was something about getting away from the office and working with people with different sorts of priorities that was tremendously inspiring, and made me view my own work differently. I was grateful for the opportunity to give something to the community, and I've got really involved with our pro bono activity since.'

These activities are worth doing in and of themselves, of course, but they offer you a new perspective. Your organization is part of a wider community, and that community may well provide you with new contacts and perspectives that you can take back into the office.

MAKE A WIDER CHARITABLE CONTRIBUTION

Charles was doing fine in his job at a large engineering firm. He turned up every day, did his job, and went largely unnoticed by anyone other than his immediate team. All that changed when, on the back of a family bereavement, he got involved in a cancer charity.

'I met up with people from different walks of life and they were all going on about the charitable work their firms did and I thought, well, we don't do anything. So I went and talked to people internally that I'd never spoken to before – I didn't know we had an events team, for example – and I spoke to the senior management and we came up with this idea of sponsoring a fun run. They were very enthusiastic but they were also, you know, "You take this, own it" – which I did. And the thing was a huge success, and it has now become an annual event. I'm more proud of it than anything else I've done – because it's in the memory of my brother – but, yes, it has done my career a lot of good. I met people I'd never have dreamed of talking to before, and it has given me an opportunity to showcase my organizational ability. My profile is high around the business, and I've just had my second promotion.'

What seems to impress people these days is someone going the extra mile – doing something that is not necessarily in their job description, is not motivated out of pure self-interest and really does require plenty of blood, sweat and tears. The motivating force in each of these examples was entirely altruistic – people had something they were passionate about and they found an opportunity to demonstrate that passion at work, not through the official day job, but by other means. And the irony is that it is possible to acquire more profile and influence from these activities than from the actual work you are paid to do.

- What voluntary opportunities are there for getting involved in something new in your workplace?
- How involved in the local community are you?
- What charitable work does your organization sponsor? Can you contribute more, or make a suggestion about a new idea?

24 Improve your performance

ᏟᏟ *'Champions keep playing until they get it right.'* Billie Jean King

ᏟᏟ *'The difference between failure and success is doing a thing nearly right and doing it exactly right.'* Edward C. Simmons

ᏟᏟ *'There's not been one radical change. A lot of it is minor details. But if you pick ten small things to work on and change, that can turn into a big difference.'* Andy Murray, on working with coach Ivan Lendl

ᏟᏟ *'True intuitive expertise is learned from prolonged experience with good feedback on mistakes.'* Daniel Kahneman

ᏟᏟ *'A successful person is one who can lay a firm foundation with the bricks that others throw at him or her.'* David Brinkley

How seriously do you take performance improvement? Do you have any clear sense of whether you are producing better work today than you did this time last year? If the answer to the second question is no – as for most of us it must be – you are severely undermining your chances of being influential. If you are not improving, there are only two other possibilities: you are maintaining level, which implies a plateau, or you are on the slide.

If you want to base your influence on the quality of your execution of a skill or your delivery of a product, you need a system in place for delivering timely and accurate feedback. Otherwise, it's all guesswork and possibly self-delusion. Unfortunately, many of us rely on the annual appraisal for our feedback, or abide by the mantra that, as far as our own performance is concerned, no news is good news.

There is much to be learned from professional sport in terms of performance enhancement. In sport, the difference between winning and losing often hangs on the smallest of margins. And unlike other walks of life, in sport there is no comfort zone where survival is guaranteed regardless of results. It is a ruthless world, where coming first is all that matters, and therefore professional sports stars and their coaching teams are meticulous about the need for continuous improvement. This means that *every* performance is debriefed and reviewed in microscopic detail; and no aspect of mind, body and spirit is overlooked in the quest for perfection. A multinational conglomerate probably takes less time analysing its own performance than a top tennis star or football team.

If we are going to take our own performance improvement seriously, we need to put in place three things:

- a reliable means of receiving regular feedback
- a mindset that is open to hearing the bad news as well as the good
- the discipline to implement the improvements necessary to take our performance to the next level.

And if that sounds like hard work, it's probably the reason why there are so few world champions, in sport or in life.

GET THE FEEDBACK

One of the complaints I hear most often from people not satisfied with their lot in organizations is that they don't get enough feedback. When I enquire whether they have *asked* for more feedback, I am met with a confused look. It isn't my job to ask for feedback, is the subtext; it's my manager's to give it to me. To which my response is: who stands to benefit the most from timely and effective feedback? If it's you, then surely it's worth taking the initiative?

Dev, an IT consultant, found this out for himself:

'I was working long hours but not getting any sense of how I was doing. I am quite competitive, and I'm motivated by getting better at something. I felt after a few months that I was just stagnating. But I really had to keep on at more senior people – they often want to just palm you off with "It's fine. You're doing fine." And I had to say "Look, I want the specifics, I want to know exactly how I am doing, and exactly what I need to do to get better." And to be fair, one or two did start to respond, and as a result I did feel like I was making progress.'

Early feedback is critical if you are starting a business as well as a new job. The whole premise of the 'lean start-up' philosophy, as popularized by Eric Ries and others, is that the more feedback a business receives in its initial phase, the easier it is to know whether to carry on or abort.

LOOK AT PROCESS, NOT OUTCOMES

Getting the feedback is the first stage, but it needs to be feedback about the right things. Sports coaches often talk about looking at the process rather than the outcomes: the fact that you did or did not score a goal is only of fleeting interest to the coach. Much more relevant is *how* the goal is scored – whether the process can be broken down into constituent actions that can each be individually analysed, practised and potentially repeated in a live match.

Dave Brailsford, the coach of the tremendously successful British Olympic cycling team, attributes much of the team's success to the 'aggregation of marginal gains'. By breaking down each of the actions that contribute to a successful cycling performance – even to the level of considering the pillows the cyclists slept on during preparation for a race – Brailsford was able to suggest incremental improvements to each of those actions that – aggregated – made the difference between victory and defeat.

In the aftermath of a meeting or presentation, we will often make a sweeping value judgement: it went well; it was a disaster. But how often will we anatomize victory or defeat – actually strive to understand what specific behaviours or processes made the difference between the one and the other?

The great sports stars and their coaches have this down pat: improvement does not come from good intentions or wishful thinking. It comes from the almost scientific application of data-driven feedback.

RITUALIZE YOUR PREPARATIONS SO THAT YOU CAN EXECUTE WHEN IT MATTERS WITHOUT THINKING

This is the holy grail of sports coaching. In practice, the basics of performance are stripped to their essentials and then honed and grooved so that they can be repeated without thought, even in the pressure-cooker atmosphere of a big match.

There is an element of ritual about the way, say, Rafa Nadal prepares for a big match. He arrives in the dressing room and takes a cold shower. He then tapes his racket handles, all six of them. He meticulously affixes his trademark bandanna. And only then does he proceed to the court, where his first action is to pick out his family members in the auditorium before placing his two water bottles beside him, labels facing the court.

This behaviour could be considered weird or pedantic. Yet it springs from an attempt to codify and formalize the ingredients of success. The mind, under pressure, can be easily distracted, by nerves or the thought of failure. Put a routine in place in practice that you can adopt in matchplay, and you remove an important variable that might affect the result.

Another key area of a sports star's preparation is in the area of self-talk. What does the golfer say to himself as he steps up to take that final putt? What runs through the batter's mind as the bowler starts her run in? An army of sports psychologists accompany every major team, and this is one of their chief responsibilities. Nothing is left to chance in the preparation – especially a player's thought process.

Of course, in business and in everyday life, we rarely get the chance to put in any practice, far less consider the intricacies of ritual à la Nadal. But the ratio of time spent practising a skill versus executing it in professional sport is around 10:1.

Maybe there's a lesson here for the rest of us?

Performance improvement in the world of sport – and, psychologists such as Daniel Kahneman suggest, in any other area of life – is painstaking, meticulous and planned. In life, most of us have good intentions, but we tend to settle for 'good enough'. If you were to treat the next six months in the way a sportsman treats the new season, how much better could you be?

- What process do you have in place to deliver timely, trusted feedback?
- If you were asked to name the dozen or so key actions that contribute most to the successful execution of your role, what would your answer be?
- How much time do you spend preparing or rehearsing for the big events?

25 Subtract and simplify

> 'We often plough so much energy into the big picture, we forget the pixels.' Silvia Cartwright

> 'Excess generally causes reaction, and produces a change in the opposite direction, whether it be in the seasons, or in individuals, or in governments.' Plato

> 'Three Rules of Work: Out of clutter find simplicity; From discord find harmony; In the middle of difficulty lies opportunity.' Albert Einstein

> 'That's been one of my mantras – focus and simplicity. Simple can be harder than complex: you have to work hard to get your thinking clean to make it simple. But it's worth it in the end because, once you get there, you can move mountains.' Steve Jobs

> 'One reason so few of us achieve what we truly want is that we never direct our focus; we never concentrate our power. Most people dabble their way through life, never deciding to master anything in particular.' Tony Robbins

Sculpture is unique among art forms in that it is essentially about subtraction rather than addition. Michelangelo famously said that every block of stone already has a statue within it. The job of the sculptor is to free it from the surrounding clutter.

This aesthetic does not fit with the times. Although we may like to think we are all minimalists now – Zen Habits, for example, is one of the most heavily subscribed blogs on the web – this does not seem to translate to the way we lead our daily lives. We all want our say. We all want in on the act. We are surrounded by the cacophony of a million online voices, largely talking to themselves. Ego dictates that if we are not 'making a contribution' we don't really exist.

In this context, there may be an opportunity to be influential by reducing the amount of clutter in life: bureaucratic, interpersonal and psychological. By having the mentality of 'What can I remove?' rather than 'What can I add?' you may make a significant contribution to productivity, your own and your organization's.

At a personal level, your productivity may be impeded by too many irrelevant demands on your time. At an organizational one, extraneous layers of 'stakeholders' may make decision making convoluted; perhaps it takes too long to respond effectively to ever-changing markets. In all areas of life there is too much communication.

It's striking that most of the great business model innovations of recent times have been, in effect, studies in subtraction, from Toyota's legendary 'just-in-time' innovations in the 1960s (reducing inventory) to Dell's approach to assembling PCs on demand, thereby eliminating the need for a retailer. Low-cost airlines have shown that by reducing the number of frills on offer, and thus the cost to the consumer, they can steal market share from the traditional carriers with their hot towels, silver service and higher overheads.

It's counterintuitive, but probably true. If you want to be more influential, don't just think of the grand intervention or the moment of inspiration. Instead, cast a critical eye over every area of your life and ask whether all that stuff really needs to be there.

CUT THE RED TAPE

Alain de Botton, in his book *The Pleasures and Sorrows of Work* (2009), suggests that the true nature of bureaucracy can best be seen in developing countries, where 'the full complement of documents, files, veneered desks and cabinets ... conveys the strict and inverse relationship between productivity and paperwork.'

Where are the bureaucratic blockages in your own system? Has a critical analysis been undertaken of whether a process aids an outcome, or undermines it?

A business development director at a large professional services firm hints at the advantages of setting people free from time-consuming bureaucracy:

'We installed this expensive Client Relationship Management system and, to justify the expense, we set out lengthy rules about how every contact with clients had to be logged and annotated, pretty much on pain of death. There were two results of this: one, the people who were good at client relations just got on with it and didn't bother to tell anyone anything. And, secondly, the people for whom this was a bit of a stretch used the complexity of the system as an excuse to do nothing. So the system we invested in to improve client relations actually reduced the amount of useable client intelligence we ended up receiving. So I cut the requirement to report all interactions – I wished I could have cut the whole system – and we started to see people use common sense to record stuff that mattered and not waste time on stuff that didn't.'

GET TO THE POINT

There is a time and a place for 'blue sky thinking'. Every day, and everywhere, is not it.

Take responsibility for keeping people on track in meetings and on calls. Have a finely tuned 'digression detector'. You don't need to be abrasive – a fairly subtle 'Are we moving off the point here?' will often suffice – but by limiting off-task chatter you will earn the gratitude of all the other participants who were thinking the same but didn't have the guts to intervene and say so.

A client we work with makes it clear that she will not respond to email messages that contain more than three bullet points, maintaining that any more than that shows a lack of focus and is likely to waste her time. She adheres religiously to the rule herself, believing that one of the main contributions she can make to her team's productivity is to reduce the amount of stuff they have to process from her. She reckons reducing 'windbaggery', as she calls it, saves her an hour a day.

So much communication includes extraneous information that is included for one purpose only: to cover the ass of the person who wrote it. Explode this conspiracy.

Demonstrate concision in your own communication, and convey that you expect it from others.

SAY NO MORE OFTEN

One of the most effective ways of reducing clutter in your own and other people's lives is to butt out more often. Ask to be taken off mailing lists. Decline that invitation to a meeting where your presence is not strictly required. Focus your time on the stuff that matters and work hard to cut out the distractions.

Some people judge their influence by how many pies they manage to stick a finger in. But is ubiquity really where it's at? The people who moan the most about double bookings and chaotic inboxes are often the ones who would moan even more loudly if they were not included. But perhaps they dilute their brand – can you think of candidates in your own circle who always seem to be present but rarely deliver anything of value?

Limit your appearances to the occasions where you can make a real contribution. This will mean getting used to saying no, but will increase your chances of impressing when you do put in an appearance. And it will free up your time to focus on your own priorities rather than be a slave to other people's.

Putting it all together

Instead of joining the jaded majority who moan about overload, why don't you take the lead in doing something about it? Rediscover the important distinction between the essential, the desirable and the irrelevant. Set the example, free others from the burden of excess, and win everybody's approval and admiration.

- Which processes seem to complicate rather than clarify? Which can you cull?
- How concise is your own communication style, in person and in email? Which meetings can you reasonably extricate yourself from?
- Can you say no to people more than you do? Practise doing it … today!

26 Share what you know

'Back, you know, a few generations ago, people didn't have a way to share information and express their opinions efficiently to a lot of people. But now they do. Right now, with social networks and other tools on the Internet, all of these 500 million people have a way to say what they're thinking and have their voice be heard.' Mark Zuckerburg

'In today's environment, hoarding knowledge ultimately erodes your power. If you know something very important, the way to get power is by actually sharing it.' Joseph Baradacco

'Knowledge is power, which is why people who had it in the past often tried to make a secret of it. In post-capitalism, power comes from transmitting information to make it productive, not from hiding it.' Peter F. Drucker

'If you have knowledge, let others light their candles in it.' Margaret Fuller

'Alchemists turned into chemists when they stopped keeping secrets.' Eric Raymond

The Internet, of course, changed everything. Back in the Dark Ages (circa 1995), one of the best ways of gaining influence was to follow this process:

1. Gain specialist knowledge or expertise.
2. Keep it to yourself.

3. Sell small portions of it to the highest bidder.
4. Repeat, with diminishing returns, until retirement.

This is essentially a 'scarcity' mentality. Cultivate something (specialist knowledge) that is in short supply and then peddle it endlessly.

This no longer works, because the prevalence of the Internet in our lives has created an 'abundance' mentality. The Internet is both an abundant resource – everything you need to know is out there somewhere, provided you have the time to look for it – but also an abundance philosophy. Greater value is placed on selflessly adding to the sum of human knowledge, on contributing freely to the conversation, than on sitting under a sign marked 'expert' and waiting for the punters to show up.

Experience and knowledge today are virtually worthless unless shared. Even then, you may not profit financially from the sharing. You will, however, begin to gain traction as an influencer, because the more you contribute to the discussion and share your expertise, the higher your profile will be.

Knowledge sharing matters in the 'real' world, of course, but it is best facilitated online. We have probably reached the stage where, if you don't have a significant online presence, you are unlikely to be a true influencer. 'Online presence' here doesn't mean a flashy website – it means the regular participation in dialogue through social media, a willingness to share your experience and insight for the benefit of others.

It is instructive to look at the blogging world for clues to how to become an influential online presence. There is a theme that unites the A-listers – other than gender and nationality – from Seth Godin to Tim Ferriss to Pat Flynn. These individuals have acquired a mega-audience by the sharing – week in, week out – of awesome content. And what makes their content awesome? It is not self-indulgent ramblings about what they watched on TV last night or their latest iTunes download. Their content takes their own insight and experience and packages it in a highly practical way for the benefit of the reader. Whether your interest is in marketing or leading an alternative lifestyle or launching a website that makes money, these people can be relied upon to offer experience-based insight and advice for free.

Whether online or off, then, what you know matters, and who you know matters even more. But a willingness to share both knowledge and contacts reaps the best return of all.

JOIN THE ONLINE DISCUSSION

Whatever your field of expertise, there will be online discussion opportunities around it. Whether it is through a LinkedIn community, a blog or a chatroom, the Internet will provide opportunities for you to connect and share with others in your field. You know this already, of course, and probably spend a bit of time every day looking at what other people have written, agreeing or disagreeing with them in your head, before getting back to work. This makes you a lurker, not an influencer. Next time, why not post a comment or share a link others may have missed? Why not ask or answer a question? And if frustration reaches boiling point and you feel people are just missing out on a crucial niche or angle, why not launch your own blog?

Best of all, if you can help people achieve something they desperately want to by sharing your expertise, do so in the most helpful, voluminous way possible. Helping others achieve their goals is a sure-fire way of building a trusted profile and gaining influence. Money may even follow. As Pat Flynn, creator of the top-rated website Smart Passive Income puts it:

'When I first started my blog back in 2008, I never intended to make any money from it. Over time, however, the SPI community has grown and as a by-product of being helpful and giving away as much as possible, I started earning from this site, too.'

As Pat publishes his monthly income figures on the site, it is possible to quantify just how successful 'being helpful' and 'giving away' has been for him. At the time of writing, his monthly income hovers around the $60,000 mark.

MASTER THE COMPELLING 'WAR STORY'

While the online world occupies much of our thinking, experience shared face to face can be even more powerful. From the moment you start a new job or enter a new phase of life, you accumulate a wealth of experience that, if collated and communicated, could be of huge value to those who follow in your path. The problem is remembering to remember it. With busy lives, our tendency is to get through each day as unscathed as possible and consign it to history as soon as our heads hit the pillow. This is to let valuable experience slip through our fingers, which other people, not to mention ourselves, can learn from.

The discipline of taking stock of successes and failures and turning them into short 'war stories' ('This was the situation – this is what I did – this is what I learned from it') doesn't have to take long, and communicating such experience to others can be both inspiring and reassuring. The failures are often more riveting than the successes. Watch what happens to attention levels when you include the words 'Let me share with you a recent disaster' in a presentation!

FACILITATE KNOWLEDGE SHARING BETWEEN OTHERS

Even in the unlikely event that you don't have unique insight and experience to share, you can still gain influence by creating a forum for others to air theirs. One of the most frequent moans heard in organizations is that internal communication – between colleagues, teams and departments – is woeful.

How can you help? From 'curating' an intranet to organizing a social event or hosting an informal 'lunch and learn' session, you will invariably receive plaudits for bringing people closer together to share and compare.

The concept of 'curation', by the way, is often applied to some of the most influential blogging sites. The skill of these bloggers lies not so much in the creation of new content as in the commissioning and co-ordination of it.

Create or curate? It's your decision.

Putting it all together

You may be surprised at how quickly the simple sharing of what you already know can gain you a following. The key is your motivation: to turn an instant profit will devalue your brand. To be of genuine help and assistance to others will enhance it.

The secret lies in organizing your experience so that it can be communicated succinctly, identifying appropriate online and offline channels, and ensuring that plenty of others join the conversation.

- When did you last share your insight or experience?
- Could people learn from your mistakes?
- What opportunities are there for you to create a forum in which people can share their experiences?

27 Implement change – but slowly

> 'Never argue; in society nothing must be discussed. Give only results.' Benjamin Disraeli

> 'It must be considered that there is nothing more difficult to carry out, nor more doubtful of success, than to initiate a new order of things.' Niccolò Machiavelli

> 'Tradition becomes our security, and when the mind is secure it is in decay.' Jiddu Krishnamurti

> 'The secret of change is to focus all of your energy not on fighting the old but on building the new.' Socrates

One of the key distinguishing features of influential people is that they have a concrete track record of accomplishment. They have done things – whereas everyone else merely talks about doing things or makes no contribution at all. But look closer and what is really remarkable is that often their early achievements were accomplished without power; it was the early track record of achievement that **led to influence**, not existing influence that enabled achievement.

How, then, to establish a track record for implementation early in your career – without the advantages of rank or line authority – which will mark you out as a 'doer' rather than a 'dreamer'?

This is risky territory. As a newcomer or a junior, the status quo is ranged powerfully against you: tweak its nose and it may chew your face off. We can probably all think of a precocious newcomer to a class, an organization or a team who started rocking the boat on arrival. His suggestions for improving things were as overwhelming as his obvious contempt for the way we've managed to get by without him for so long. The chances are he didn't last long. The forces of conservatism moved in for the kill. Keep always in mind the fact that no one likes a know-all.

The other classic approach is less toxic but just as self-destructive. The newcomer adopts a 'wait and see' policy that morphs into a 'came and went' opportunity. The bright and enthusiastic defer to the pale and stale. 'Things could be different round here but it's not my place to act – I'll leave it till later/I'll leave it to my boss/I'll leave it till I'm asked.'

Getting things done when you are new and less experienced requires tact and subtlety – but it is a great predictor of future success.

RESPECT (SOME) TRADITIONS

As in the example above, nothing is likely to be more injurious to your chance of implementing change and gaining influence than an attempt to move too fast too soon. When you first move into a new team, role or organization, there must be a period of acclimatization, of reconnaissance. You will achieve high levels of approval and lay the ground for change by appreciating the best of the existing regime. Traditions must be observed before they can be broken.

Spend time with 'elder statesmen' purely to listen to their stories. Go to the Christmas party. Find out about the history of the place, and reference that history whenever you can. Look through the news archive. Get used to the jargon, the acronyms, the nicknames, and start to use them.

You don't want to take things too far, of course. Asking questions and expressing a divergent opinion are perfectly reasonable. But a period of immersion in the culture you have just joined is a sensible investment of time: it shows respect and wins some too.

Sports stars are particularly good at 'getting' the tradition bit. A professional football coach recalls the manager he most respected in his playing days:

'On his first day he spent a lot of time looking at the trophy cabinet and talking to the ground staff, most of whom had been around for donkey's years. It was low key, but it has stayed in my head as a very dignified way to start a new job.'

START SMALL

So you've paid your dues, shown your respect and are now itching to change things. Again, caution is required. Rather than attempting anything too ambitious, you would be best advised to start with something small and low profile. It is difficult to recover from an opening gambit that goes disastrously wrong in the full glare of public attention.

Maybe you want to improve a process or introduce a new approach. Play down expectations. Draw a couple of people into your confidence and outline what you want to try. Let them voice any concerns but also, you hope, agree to be guinea pigs. Try your idea out with a small group of people, see how it goes and take seriously any kind of negative feedback or consequences. Get your teething troubles out of the way before they can do your reputation any kind of damage.

Alan, a marketing professional in a large international organization, set out his stall for change in just this way:

'I was concerned that we weren't responsive enough to our clients, that there was basically a mindset of, "Do the work, send the invoice, move on." Some of our contracts are worth hundreds of thousands, so I thought this was a bit inadequate. I decided on virtually a "laboratory" approach. Just with individual accounts, single projects, I tried different things. One was a quick call at the end of the project; another was a short online questionnaire. I'd just observe the responses – some got none at all, others got negative responses. But this simple traffic-light idea – where we just got in touch with a simple email with red, green and amber buttons which the client would press according to how happy he was with the assignment – got lots of positives. So I very slowly rolled it out to other accounts, and only when I was certain it was a winner did I take it forward.'

Starting an 'idea lab' in your personal fiefdom is the way to go – innovate, experiment, hone. When you take it to the next level, it's not an idea you are pitching but a tried and tested improvement.

PITCH THE RESULT, NOT YOURSELF

To gain influence out of making a change or an innovation, you need to get recognition for it at a senior level. Once you have perfected the improvement in your 'lab', the time has come to take it to the boardroom.

The one cardinal rule here is: avoid self-promotion. You must not seem to be making a play for recognition. You must present the results of your laboratory exactly as a scientist would: with the facts, in detail, and preferably corroborated by peer review.

In Alan's case above, he put an item on the agenda of the next partnership meeting with the title 'Client Feedback Report'. Everyone was interested in what clients had to say, so his item was eagerly anticipated. He presented the facts without embellishment: average client satisfaction score in the control group: 6.8; average score with the traffic-light system: 8.9. Then he showed a short extract of an interview he had filmed with one of the happy clients, who said:

'I liked this because it was simple to use, came at a great time, and meant that little issues could be addressed on the go before they reached critical proportions. Simple idea, but I've not seen it before. Well done.'

The managing partner nodded approval. 'Why haven't we thought of doing this before?' he said. 'Was it your idea, Alan?'

Alan nodded. 'I came up with it, but it was my team who put it into action.'

'Well done, then. Let's implement across the firm and, Alan, can you lead on it?'

This shows a textbook example of influence achieved by deeds, not words.

Change, rather like a visit to the dentist, is something we know is good for us but would rather it happened to other people. Your ability to implement change – be it transformative or incremental – is certainly one of the keys to acquiring greater influence. The challenge is to do it in the right way, bringing everyone with you. Crashing and burning, or creating so much resentment that you surround yourself with enemies, are clearly counterproductive. But don't be put off – slowly and steadily is the way to win this particular race.

- Where have you publicly embraced some of the traditions of a culture you are planning to change?
- What ideas could profit from the 'idea lab' approach?
- How confident are you about selling your ideas on their merits to senior stakeholders?

28 Replenish

'Remember, if you don't do anything – if you don't change the way your mind works and direct your subconscious mind to create the life you want – then everything stays the same, nothing changes.' Steve Backley

'Spirit does not belong to any particular religion because It has nothing to do with any religion and humanity cannot claim any exclusivity to It because we and our planet are nothing but a drop in the ocean of this endless universe.' Thomas Vazhakunnathu

'The yoga mat is a good place to turn when talk therapy and anti-depressants aren't enough.' Amy Weintraub

'True silence is the rest of the mind, and is to the spirit what sleep is to the body, nourishment and refreshment.' William Penn

'In Kabbalah, as in the Hassidic tradition, you cure the body, but you fix the soul. Curing takes time, but fixing, if you know how to do it, is immediate.' Rabbi Shlomo Carlebach

Robert was a star trainee at his international law firm. He was known as 'the machine' for his ability to crank out quality work at any time of the day or night. His work rate was the envy of his peers. Partners loved him because he didn't complain about antisocial hours or work–life balance; he just, in the parlance of the firm, 'sucked it up'. He was on the fast track to partnership, maybe before he was 30. Then one day, his colleagues arrived in the office to find not Robert but a small handwritten note sitting at his desk. 'Can't cope. Sorry.' And with those three words a stellar legal career came to an end. Robert never came back to the office, and he was last heard of doing temporary work for a charity, where the pay was poor but the pressure more manageable.

This is hardly an isolated story. Most of us will know of people who burned out, dropped out, or worse. The trouble with the talented or the industrious is that they are particularly susceptible to the myth of personal elasticity: that no matter what stresses or strains we put on ourselves, we will always bounce back, always have more in the tank.

This is delusional. To be genuinely influential, we need to be able to sustain a level of high performance over a period of time; the influential are not, generally, here today and gone tomorrow. To sustain that performance, we need to maintain optimal levels of personal resource: physical, spiritual and intellectual. These all expire over time, and it is your job to notice when the levels are low, and to go about replenishing them.

Energy is finite, even for the young, and needs to be replenished.

The level of personal accountability is striking in all the influential people I've worked with and interviewed for this book. Many of us might mortgage our wellbeing to other people: for example, 'The boss will look after me, he'll know when I've had enough.' Sadly, this is seldom true. You are best placed to take account of your personal resources (too low is too late) and for ensuring their replenishment.

For those of you who think the candle is for burning at both ends, beware – and read on.

GET MOVING

It's striking that every single person I interviewed for this book – who had all attained levels of influence in their spheres – took exercise seriously. It was virtually the only common denominator. The interpretation of the word varied: some were at the hardcore end of Ironman challenges and 100-kilometre hikes;

others tried to fit in 30 minutes in the gym a couple of times a week. Whatever the approach or the intensity, I was struck by the fact that exercise didn't only offer these people an opportunity to fight flab and build physical fitness; it offered a breathing space, an opportunity to think. For these people, the 'third space' in their lives after home and work is not a coffee shop but the gym. One manager commented:

'When I need to do some serious thinking, I always get out of the office. I'll go for a walk around the park next to our building – not an amble, a fairly rapid walk – or in bad weather I'll go to the gym. I find that the different environment, the exercise, the energy gives me space to think. Sure, the exercise is good for me. But I rarely make great decisions sitting behind my desk. Removing myself to somewhere different is key.'

Fitting exercise into a busy working week is, of course, a challenge. But where there's a will…

'I started getting off the Tube a few stops early, just so that I get an hour's physical exercise in every day,' said Sarah, an HR specialist. 'And I even got one of those foldaway bikes to take on the train. I'd have to spend the time commuting anyway; I figured I may as well multitask and get some exercise into the bargain.'

DIVERSIFY YOUR FRAMES OF REFERENCE

The same people and the same issues: after you've been in the same place for a while, staleness can become inevitable. This is why it is important to keep your intellectual environment stimulating as well as varying your physical environment, to keep ennui at bay.

The next time you buy a magazine, choose one you've never read before. Next time you're downloading a podcast, check out some categories you wouldn't normally visit. Likewise, chose different TV programmes and music or even a different route to work. It's amazing, given the multiplicity of information available to us, that as schedulers of our own lifestyle channel, we tend to be pretty conservative, as Ian who heads up a finance function explains:

'My reading was mostly limited to the big news sites, which I used primarily to keep up to date with sports results. But on a whim at an airport I bought one of these tech magazines and became intrigued by an article on Google. The piece was about the whole idea of "office hours" – where some of the top execs set aside time every week when people can just sign up and come and meet with them on a first come, first served basis. And I thought, wow, we could do that. And it has been really popular. I just never would have come up with that sort of idea if I hadn't picked up the mag. It's not a new idea in the tech industry, I guess, but for us it was revolutionary.'

CULTIVATE DISTRACTIONS

It was famously said of Margaret Thatcher that she 'had no hinterland'. Her life was politics, which made her frame of reference fairly narrow, and she was said to find it nearly impossible to switch off and relax.

By contrast, researchers into resilience have found that consciously cultivating distractions – areas of life not connected with work – are critically important in helping people replenish their energy and, paradoxically, concentrate all the better at work.

What are the pleasurable distractions in your life? We have discussed exercise. Maybe it is family life, travel or sport. For many top-ranking individuals, it is charitable work. John, the CEO of an environmental consultancy, puts it like this:

'You have to get some perspective in your life. When you are in a position of influence, you start to become consumed by the role, by the politics, by the business. For me, helping out at a local care home is an important release. I realize how fortunate I am to live the life I do, and also see the problems I deal with as being negligible when compared to the work of full-time carers and the lives of people coping with disabilities. I also volunteer overseas at least once every three years. Get out of your ivory tower, that's my advice to anyone who wants to retain their sanity in positions of authority.'

Putting it all together

People sometimes realize, too late, when their intellectual, physical or spiritual reserves have run dangerously low. They then run the risk of being better known for a spectacular 'crash and burn' than for their creativity or contribution. By taking stock of your own energy levels and having strategies in place to replenish them when required, you stay fresh – an overlooked but critical aspect of staying influential.

- Do you incorporate physical exercise into your weekly schedule? How easy is it for you to physically change location – walk around the block, for example – when you are feeling stressed?
- When did you last access a new source of information? What have you done today for the first time?
- How broad are your interests outside work? What do you do to 'get away from it all'? Who or what do you rely on to give you a sense of perspective?

Part 4

Who you are: influence
through personal impact

29 Know your strengths

'At Facebook, we try to be a strengths-based organization, which means we try to make jobs fit around people rather than make people fit around jobs. We focus on what people's natural strengths are and spend our management time trying to find ways for them to use those strengths every day.' Sheryl Sandberg

'Emphasize your strengths on your résumé, in your cover letters and in your interviews. It may sound obvious, but you'd be surprised how many people simply list everything they've ever done. Convey your passion and link your strengths to measurable results. Employers and interviewers love concrete data.' Marcus Buckingham

'I know where I'm going and I know the truth, and I don't have to be what you want me to be. I'm free to be what I want.' Muhammad Ali

'A person can perform only from strength. One cannot build performance on weaknesses.' Peter Drucker

'I spend a lot of time talking to people about what they're good at and how we make that better, rather than areas where they're weak. That's not to say that you ignore areas of weakness, but they're not the areas where you make vast improvements. If you find things that make you different and make them super strengths, then you can see people make leaps in performance. Super strengths are the parts *of the game in which someone could potentially be the best in the world.'* Dr Mark Bawden, Head of Sports Psychology, English Institute of Sport

To be influential requires a certain level of self-confidence – not the kind of overweening arrogance that is really insecurity in heavy disguise, but a quiet confidence in one or two specific areas of skill, expertise or insight. This kind of confidence requires that you be honest about yourself – about your weaknesses, yes, but particularly about acknowledging your strengths.

What is it that makes the critic on our shoulder such a potent saboteur of so much we might have done? Maybe it's the educational system or cultural norms or any number of factors; whatever the cause, many of us are more conscious of our shortcomings than our strengths. Take, for example, Anna, an office worker who received a glowing appraisal:

'Everything was positive – people management, service delivery, product knowledge – but there was this one comment about not showing flexibility, not coming forward with new ideas. And this really bugged me – I kept running it over and over in my mind. It's true that I'm not particularly creative and never have been – but it annoys me that this has been commented on and will probably put a ceiling on my career.'

Anna focuses entirely on a perceived weakness – which produces a sense of defeatism – rather than looking to her strengths for the answer. She already has great product knowledge, for example; perhaps she could use this as the basis for suggestions for future product development. She just needs to look at her specialist knowledge in a different way.

The influential will have a clear – but not idealized – view of their own strengths. There will be two or three areas of expertise, skill or knowledge that they acknowledge as particularly well developed and of real transferable value. It is this repository of strength that gives them the confidence to try to influence in the first place, and to which they will return when confronted by setbacks or obstacles along the way.

RECORD YOUR SUCCESSES

As children, our strengths are acknowledged all the time. The painting, the spelling test, the sports day: even modest achievement is recognized and praised and effort is rewarded. In adulthood, unless we are blessed with a particularly diligent manager or partner, the good we do often goes unnoticed. It is largely up to us to record our successes, and to figure out exactly what and how we contributed to them.

By all means seek out third-party feedback or go online and take a strengths test (Martin Seligman's at www.authentichappiness.sas. upenn.edu/Default.aspx is one of the more robust), but also take careful account of the things that you do on a day-to-day basis that get good results. Keep a detailed, written record of these success stories. Be specific: what were the actions, behaviours and processes that you implemented to achieve your goals?

Recording success in this way helps us understand themes or patterns of achievement that may become apparent only over time. And success stories are especially valuable in times of adversity; they remind us that we have a track record of success, and enable us to replay and then re-enact the types of actions that got us there.

LEVERAGE YOUR STRENGTHS

Influential people are often very skilled at identifying new opportunities for themselves – new spheres in which to thrive. The basis for this is often an acute awareness of any key strength that is transferable.

A CEO we work with has built a 30-year career zigzagging across sectors as diverse as telecoms, pharmaceuticals and consumer goods.

'I'm not paid to design the products. I'm paid to build a high-performing team that executes our strategy and makes a profit. That's about a relentless focus on the numbers and selecting and motivating the right talent, two things I'm pretty good at. Whether it's a blockbuster drug or a broadband infrastructure we're selling is ultimately irrelevant. I believe variety is the spice of life, and I've deliberately sought out varied opportunities where I can apply whatever skills I have.'

Once you have a transferable strength and a track record of successful implementation, the key is to promote and leverage that strength to open up new opportunities and challenges. And once you get a reputation for effectiveness across a range of arenas, you can become very influential indeed.

HIRE TO COMPENSATE FOR YOUR WEAKNESSES

All this is not to suggest that you don't have weaknesses; of course you do. It's just that spending time and money attempting to turn weaknesses into strengths may be a very long-term proposition and not the best use of your time. While you can embark on training programmes and university courses, read books or listen to podcasts, bringing a skill or competence up from 'poor' to 'moderate' is unlikely to increase your influence. It may be quicker simply to bring in other people who possess the skills you don't.

Tim, an entrepreneur in the food and beverage space, shared this story:

'The best thing I ever did was to bring in a professional manager. I have no head for figures at all – I love my work and I am passionate about the product but I just want to be left alone to make it. But as we grew, I found myself getting more and more bogged down in spreadsheets and projections and it was starting to destroy my creativity. My enthusiasm for the business began to wane. So bringing in Ellie [as finance director] was incredibly important. I could leave all the finance to her – because it's what she has real expertise in – and I could get back to my passion, which is brewing beer. We've never looked back.'

Overreach can be fatally damaging to reputation, which is why influencers recognize their limitations, and ensure that they have a team around them that allows them to capitalize on their signature strength and leave the rest to other people.

Putting it all together

The world of professional sport has plenty to teach us about identifying and leveraging key strengths. The route to success in sport is often about harnessing one particular skill, perfecting it, and being able to execute it impeccably under extreme pressure. David Beckham, for instance, was never the greatest header of a football, or the greatest tackler. But his passing was often inch-perfect, and he built his stellar career around the successful execution of that very specific skill in set pieces. It is noticeable that in many accounts of sporting genius, a signature skill is identified early, and the sportsman or -woman works on it obsessively over the years so that it comes to define them. Think of R.A. Dickey's knuckleball or Kevin Pietersen's switch hit.

The lesson here is that it only takes one key strength, practised and perfected to make you a world-beater.

The critical success factors seem to be a heightened awareness of what you do well, and a refusal to be sidetracked into spending too much time trying to turn yourself into something you're not.

- Can you list your three signature strengths?
- Where are they deployable, beyond your current context?
- Who compensates for your relative weaknesses with complementary strengths?

30 Speak clean

> 'Speak the speech I pray you as I pronounced it to you, trippingly on the tongue; but if you mouth it as many of your players do, I had as lief the town-crier spoke my lines. Nor do not saw the air too much with your hand thus, but use all gently; for in the very torrent, tempest, and, as I may say, whirlwind of your passion, you must acquire and beget a temperance that may give its smoothness.' William Shakespeare, *Hamlet*

> 'Speak clearly, if you speak at all; carve every word before you let it fall.' Oliver Wendell Holmes

> 'Remember not only to say the right thing in the right place, but far more difficult still, to leave unsaid the wrong thing at the tempting moment.' Benjamin Franklin

> 'If I went back to college again, I'd concentrate on two areas, learning to write and to speak before an audience. Nothing in life is more important than the ability to communicate effectively.' Gerald R. Ford

It's not fair but it is true: people equate confidence with competence, and lack of confidence with incompetence. If you seem confident in what you say, people will assume that you know what you are talking about. This means that your power to influence is to a large extent predicated on your ability to communicate with confidence.

My 15 years as a presentation coach have shown me that people have a surprising number of misconceptions when it comes to assessing what defines confident communication. Some people think it's all to do with the volume of your voice: he who shouts loudest is likely to get what he wants. Others equate confident communication with the elusive concept of 'charisma'.

I take a different view. Confident communication comes down to clarity. You need to get your message across in plain, simple language entirely free from the hesitations and digressions that habitually undermine what we want to say. We need to speak clean. This doesn't just mean we cut out the expletives, although that would be a good start. It's more that we work hard to cut out all the noise in our interpersonal communication that often obscures the signal.

When I film people in training sessions, and they watch themselves on screen during the playback, a common reaction is surprise: 'I didn't know I waffled so much...' 'I had no idea that I said "um" all the time...' 'Why am I looking down at my notes?'

We so often sabotage ourselves when we cloud our message with all this distracting behaviour. The effect is magnified in phone conversations when, without the help of body language to provide additional context, clarity is at even more of a premium.

Self-awareness is the first part of the solution. Watch some film of yourself presenting. Record a phone conversation. And once you are aware of your verbal tics, aim to eliminate them and make your communication as crystal clear as possible.

MAKE YOUR PAUSES INAUDIBLE

Picture the scene. You are in an important meeting. All the key players are assembled around the table. Everyone is invited to introduce themselves and to give their initial impression of the document under discussion. Other people give their finely tuned thoughts, then all eyes are on you. What comes out of your mouth?

'Um ... err ... well, it's err ...' With those five sounds, your ability to influence the meeting dissipates.

It's perfectly normal, of course, to hesitate sometimes, and be less than fluent. My theory is that the 'um' is your brain working in an audible pause – a microsecond of thinking time – while it orders its thoughts. There is no doubt, though, that excessive umming and erring will undermine your impact and therefore your ability to influence.

Replace the audible pause with an inaudible one – just pause. Gather your thoughts in silence. This is easier said than done and it requires real discipline. It may be worth memorizing the first line of calls or presentations – even the way you introduce yourself – just to avoid that anticlimactic opener, 'Um … err …'

UNDERSTAND THAT LESS IS MORE

No one ever walked away from a presentation saying, 'That was way too short – I wanted it to use up far more of my time.'

Give people a platform, and they often don't know when to stop. They will often say, in a blinding moment of revelation, 'I may be going off the point here,' and then proceed to hold court for the next ten minutes on something even less relevant.

Is this you? If so, you need to learn to say more with fewer words. Cut out the multiple questions, the unconscious repetitions and the irrelevant comparison or anecdote.

We mistakenly assume that expertise is best demonstrated through volume. We think that, unless we show, in mind-numbing detail, exactly how *much* we know, we will be exposed as frauds. Nothing is further from the truth: the great influencers are very rarely windbags. They understand that other people's time is as precious as their own, can distinguish between 'must-knows' and 'nice-to-knows', and are ruthless editors of their own material. They get to the point, and quickly.

Use fewer words; talk about fewer concepts; make fewer digressions. If people want to know more, they'll ask.

DON'T UNDERMINE YOUR MESSAGE

Our intention is entirely reasonable: we want to be polite and not come across as arrogant. The trouble is that, all too often, in doing so we undermine the gravity of our message.

Using qualifiers like 'perhaps', 'maybe', 'possibly' in your speech are evidence of a lack of confidence and they invite contradiction or opposition. Worst of all is 'just':

- 'I just wanted to make the point that…'
- 'I just thought it might be an idea to…'

The word implies insecurity and hesitancy, and as such is an invitation not to take the speaker seriously.

Some of this use of language is cultural. The British, a famously 'high-context' nation, are known for not saying what they mean, leaving much to subtext and interpretation. For example, saying, 'Perhaps you might possibly like to have another look at this…' might be interpreted by someone Dutch or Australian as a genuine choice. (Perhaps I would, perhaps I wouldn't.) An English person would immediately pick up that his full attention needed to be turned on the document, and fast.

Even outside the cultural context, we can often unconsciously undermine our case by using weak, redundant words and phrases when it would be more beneficial to be direct. Even when introducing themselves, some individuals assume an apologetic tone: 'I'm David,' I once heard an individual say at the start of a meeting, 'You probably won't be interested in what I've got to say.'

Another telltale sign of insecurity is when people begin speaking despite the fact that others in the room are not listening. A confident speaker would always insist on quiet before proceeding: she has something important to impart, so why would she open her mouth when people are not giving her their full attention?

It is very difficult to influence when everything about our tone, our vocabulary and our demeanour screams out that we don't even take ourselves seriously.

Putting it all together

Impact and influence are obviously closely linked, and it is difficult to make an impact when we are intent on sabotaging ourselves. Sound confident and people will listen. The trouble is that we often get into self-defeating patterns in our communication style where, without realizing it, we are severely restricting our chances of engaging an audience. This can be rectified: confidence, unlike knowledge or skill or expertise, can be faked. The right body language, the right tone and a pragmatic choice of what to include and what to leave out can create aligned, impactful communication that stands a chance of persuading and influencing the target audience.

- When did you last see or hear yourself present?
- Can you replace any ums or distracting verbal tics with a pause?
- Can you try using shorter sentences and getting to the point more quickly?

Eliminate qualifiers like 'perhaps' and 'maybe' from your lexicon. The audience won't take you seriously if you seem unsure about your right to speak.

31 Stay fresh

> 'A human being should be able to change a diaper, plan an invasion, butcher a hog, conn a ship, design a building, write a sonnet, balance accounts, build a wall, set a bone, comfort the dying, take orders, give orders, co-operate, act alone, solve equations, analyse a new problem, pitch manure, program a computer, cook a tasty meal, fight efficiently, die gallantly. Specialization is for insects.' **Robert A. Heinlein**

> 'Models now need to promote themselves, think like businesswomen and diversify their careers by doing other things. Chances are very slim that a mere model will become a household name today.' **Tyra Banks**

> 'You can only ride on your medals so long. Your athletics career might finish at 30, then the rest of your life starts.' **Frankie Fredericks, Olympic sprinter**

> 'I refuse to be typecast, and I'll have a go at anything so long as it's different, challenging, hard work and demands great versatility.' **Pete Postlethwaite**

> 'Business opportunities are like buses, there's always another one coming.' **Richard Branson**

Anyone in the happy position of having wealth to invest will have been told over and over: diversify your portfolio. Don't keep all your money in stocks, the experts will tell you, because stocks are extremely volatile. Don't keep all your money in cash under a mattress, because inflation will nibble away at it. Don't keep all your money in bonds or fixed-interest accounts, because you'll fail to capitalize on an upswing in the economy. By diversifying, you share your money around a bit and you don't get too exposed to any one asset class.

This makes a lot of sense well beyond the realm of personal finance. Why would you ever put all your eggs in one basket and run the risk that you might lose the lot?

Well, most of us do. We get a vague hunch about the kind of thing we want to do in life, and doggedly plough that furrow with varying degrees of enthusiasm for most of our adult lives. For all the talk of portfolio careers, the 'one job' mentality – particularly in a time when jobs are scarce – is still pretty pervasive. This is a high-risk strategy, however – with the risks ranging from obsolescence to plain old staleness.

Our potency, our reach and our longevity would all benefit from some kind of hedging strategy – an approach that would see our influence transcend career culs-de-sac and to some extent protect us from the vagaries of the market.

How does diversify sit with specialize, the subject of an earlier chapter? The two ideas are not as contradictory as they seem. For example, Richard Branson, whose business empire must be among the most diversified ever created, didn't just 'dabble' in the music business before starting his airline; he nailed it. And having nailed it, he moved on: there were new worlds to conquer. So perhaps diversification is actually serial specialization – not allowing yourself to be confined by a particular skillset or one area of expertise, but staying one step ahead, forever in motion.

Here are three possible areas of diversification that could enhance your influence: challenges, platforms and networks.

KEEP THE NEXT CHALLENGE IN VIEW AS YOU APPROACH A PLATEAU

Many career paths, especially the better-paid ones, require a lengthy apprenticeship. Years are spent studying, observing and practising until the wonderful day comes when we are qualified to do whatever we set out to. It's an interesting paradox, then, that the arrival sometimes isn't as fulfilling as the journey. Once we get over the elation of 'passing' and settle down into the business of putting into practice what we have struggled so hard to attain, there is a distinct fork in the road: we can opt for complacency and possible staleness or further challenge and reinvigoration.

A law firm partner told us:

'I'd been working all this time to make partner, putting in all these crazy hours. I had been driven and focused on this for eight, nine years. And then I made it, and the wind sort of went out of my sails. I thought, "Now what?" It was a real anti-climax. And I looked around at some of my fellow partners who looked old and stale and utterly cynical and I thought, "Is that me in ten years' time?"'

Complacency can be warded off in one of two ways, both of which involve a measure of diversification. New challenges need to be found within the role, or alternative realities envisioned. The same partner opted for the first strategy:

'I didn't want to be one of those stale old sods just taking the money. So, once I felt I knew the ropes, I started looking for new responsibilities: one new area a year. I got involved in graduate recruitment, then opening up a new office. I consciously change the role every year to keep myself fresh.'

Sometimes more drastic changes are required, or imposed in the case of professional sport, which has such a short window for peak performance. One former professional sportsman consciously developed a parallel career as a psychotherapist, which became full time when his sporting career was over.

'I didn't want to be one of those sad pros who live off their memories on the after-dinner circuit. I'm actually more influential as a psychotherapist with a sporting background than I would have been as a has-been kicking around the training ground.'

DIVERSIFY YOUR PLATFORM

We speak about the need to self-promote elsewhere in the book. However you choose to do it, you will essentially be building a platform: a means of getting your message to your intended audience, be it within an organization or across the World Wide Web.

It's easy to get stuck in a rut with this. You go to the same awards ceremony or drinks events at the same time every year, for example, or you write a blog that has a loyal but stagnant readership.

By varying the channels you use to promote yourself, you stand a greater chance of building your profile and gaining more reach. So the inveterate drinks-attender might dip a toe in the water of social media. The blogger might find some mileage in looking to hold an event for her readers, or by looking to write guest posts for another blog. Maybe the podcaster should try a video, or the YouTube star an ebook.

The more diverse your promotional platform, the broader your audience is likely to be.

SEEK OUT MULTIPLE SOUNDING BOARDS

It's unusual to find an influential person, even at a senior level, who does not rely on someone else's opinion from time to time. That is not say that these people do not trust their own judgement, just that they are wise enough to know that a second opinion can be useful in terms of clarifying a decision or a course of action.

The difficulty comes when the sounding boards all sound the same. That would imply a closed circuit, where dissenting voices are shut out. Margaret Thatcher famously assessed an unfamiliar face by asking 'Is he one of us?' If the answer was in the negative, the newcomer was unlikely to be admitted to her inner sanctum. This strategy eventually isolated her from the real views of her party until there was little the yes-men could do to prolong her stay in Downing Street.

Seek advice from as wide a pool as possible. That's not to say you need to accept or act on the advice. But influence, like anything else, is difficult to sustain in a vacuum. Previous generations were wise to this: the court jester was given licence in medieval times to criticize his master severely, just so that the court be protected from absolute sycophancy.

'I always judge an incoming CEO by the company he keeps,' says a veteran City-watcher. 'How widely does he consult? The worst business decisions in the last ten years have been made by people who either didn't consult widely enough or only consulted people in their own image.'

Putting it all together

As creatures of habit, we tend to stick with what we know, but in career terms this is a dangerous strategy. Some hedging here and there, keeping options and points of view open, seems to provide a chance for influence to be sustained over a period of time rather than becoming a victim of fad or fashion.

What makes sense for your finances also has merit and application for your career, your relationships and your wider life.

- What would you do if your current role disappeared tomorrow?
- How can you extend your promotional platform?
- How varied are the sources of advice you turn to in times of trouble?

32

Don't expect the world to be logical

> 'When dealing with people, let us remember we are not dealing with creatures of logic. We are dealing with creatures of emotion, creatures bristling with prejudices and motivated by pride and vanity.' Dale Carnegie

> 'There's no evidence whatsoever that men are more rational than women. Both sexes seem to be equally irrational.' Albert Ellis

> 'Nine-tenths of tactics are certain, and taught in books: but the irrational tenth is like the kingfisher flashing across the pool, and that is the test of generals.' T. E. Lawrence

> 'When the intensity of emotional conviction subsides, a man who is in the habit of reasoning will search for logical grounds in favour of the belief which he finds in himself.' Bertrand Russell

> 'If the world were a logical place, men would ride side-saddle.' Rita Mae Brown

Imagine that you've decided to lose some weight. You've been standing on the scales with increasing trepidation for some time and now it's time for action. You invest in the latest bestselling diet book and read it from cover to cover. Next time you go shopping, you cut out all the bad stuff and fill the trolley with fruit and vegetables. The book told you all about calorific intake and, in conjunction with data about your age and current weight, you work out how many calories a day will be your maximum. The data is logical, clear and compelling: eat this number of calories and no more, together with a certain amount of exercise, and you will lose weight.

Week one goes by – slowly. The solitary poached egg for breakfast you can handle. The cauliflower soup in the evening is quite flavoursome. You tell yourself you don't even miss that visit to the sandwich shop at lunchtime that used to break up your day. Just as the data predicted, you lose a couple of pounds a week.

But then the weather turns colder and you have a particularly tough week at work. One morning the car won't start. By Friday evening, your partner says you look as if you need cheering up. A takeaway and a bottle of wine will surely do the trick.

The data is logical, clear and compelling. There are more calories in the evening's proposed food and drink than your diet allows you to eat in a week, let alone a day. The diet book is quite clear: this is all about discipline. Abide by simple rules, and reap the inevitable reward… Later that night, the worse for drink and bloated with Chinese food, you reflect that you totally deserved a treat, what's the point of being hungry and unhappy, and that this clearly wasn't the right time to think about losing weight…

We are not entirely logical creatures. Our emotions are frequently in the driving seat. It has been suggested that every purchase we make is largely done on instinct, and later justified with a selective view of the facts.

And, despite the depressing evidence of innumerable business presentations, no one can hope to influence effectively by relying on logic alone. It's the mix of logic and emotion that does the trick.

VARY THE STIMULI

Howard Gardner, the father of the theory of multiple intelligences, contends that there are eight intelligences: visual, intrapersonal, interpersonal, kinaesthetic, logical, environmental, musical and verbal. Whether you agree with all the categories or not, it's hard to resist the idea that our attention is better captured by multiple stimuli rather than just the same old approach. People crave variety.

In practice, this means that, although you probably like the sound of your own voice, your audience possibly prefers it in limited doses. Encouraging interaction in meetings and calls gets other voices involved. Handing out drawings and diagrams, and even photographs, gets the visual part of the brain engaged.

Props can be useful. They can be samples and models, or something to taste or even smell – our supermarkets have long known how to use the alluring aroma of freshly baked bread. Anything that makes your interaction memorable and less boring will likely pay a dividend in enhanced engagement.

'I quite like baking,' says Rod, a retail manager, 'and I just got into the habit of bringing in some cakes for our monthly departmental meeting. The response was crazy: people actually told me they looked forward to the meetings, and the tone of them was usually upbeat and positive. I don't attribute all of that to the brilliance of my cupcakes, but it did seem to change the mood!'

CONSIDER THEIR RECEPTIVITY TO YOUR MESSAGE

In obsessing over our message and the intricacies of our argument, we sometimes overlook the fact that our efforts to influence are undermined by extraneous factors. To receive and understand your message, an audience needs the ambience to be right.

Time of day plays a part. Do you want to strike when energy levels are at their highest – say Monday morning – or when resistance is lowest – say Friday evening? And different people are at their most receptive at different times.

'It always used to irritate me when people would come into my office and start a deep and meaningful conversation at 4 o'clock on a Wednesday when anybody who knew me recognized that that was the one day when I picked the kids up from school and I was really keen to get out on time. So people would get short shrift.'

Some people will be affected by the amount of natural light in a room, or lack of it. Others will be sensitive to temperature – too hot and the brain starts getting addled and the concentration waivers.

If you want a favourable outcome, you may as well pay some attention to ensuring that your audience is ready to engage with your message, and sometimes that comes down to simple environmental factors.

FOCUS ON WHAT THEY STAND TO LOSE

Among the many significant discoveries made by Daniel Kahneman – bestselling author of **Thinking Fast and Slow** (2011) – is his understanding of the prevalence of the completely irrational phenomenon of loss aversion. In effect, this theory proposes that people would rather not lose the £100 in their pockets than gain another £100 from another source. We put a greater value on an asset we hold than an equivalent asset somewhere else.

The implications of this effect for influence are quite profound. Whereas we might typically devote much of our time to persuading people of the benefits of our new product or strategy or innovation, attempting to entice them with the prospect of a new and better destination, the risk-aversion research would suggest that we would be better off looking at the dangers of staying where we are. What we have to lose by standing still is more powerful than what we have to gain by making the change. If we are truly to influence, we need to know what people most value, and then demonstrate how they stand to lose it. This could alter the tone of many influencing efforts, which mistakenly place too much emphasis on incentivizing an audience rather than worrying them.

This is an area that perplexes and frustrates many professionals, particularly those with a technical background. The human mind does not operate along linear, logical lines. As influencers, we can either accept this and ensure that we pay attention to the illogical, bizarre and plain infuriating ways our audiences are likely to respond to us, or carry on presenting arguments of impeccable logic that somehow never carry the day.

- What other stimuli can you use to engage, other than your own words? Pictures? Props?
- What time and location are likely to ensure maximum receptivity to your message?
- What does your audience stand to lose if they do not agree with your proposal?

(33) Learn optimism

'When one door of happiness closes, another opens; but often we look so long at the closed door that we do not see the one which has been opened for us.' Helen Keller

'A pessimist sees the difficulty in every opportunity; an optimist sees the opportunity in every difficulty.' Winston Churchill

'If you paint in your mind a picture of bright and happy expectations, you put yourself into a condition conducive to your goal.' Norman Vincent Peale

'Few things in the world are more powerful than a positive push. A smile. A word of optimism and hope. A "you can do it" when things are tough.' Richard M. DeVos

'The reason we all like to think so well of others is that we are all afraid for ourselves. The basis of optimism is sheer terror.' Oscar Wilde

Resilience has come to be recognized as a fashionable trait in leaders. We often get asked to design workshops around this concept, perhaps because leaders themselves like the associations the word has with granite-like solidity, boldly facing down the vagaries of everyday life and courage in adversity.

When we anatomize resilience, though, we find that one of its key elements is optimism. This is when our workshop designs tend to get rejected or rebuffed. Optimism, despite the long-standing and pioneering work of 'positive' psychologists, is still

169

viewed as a questionable, lightweight concept with little to offer the worrisome world of work.

And yet an optimistic mindset immediately helps someone stand out from the crowd. Moaners, whingers and doom-mongers are always in the majority, wherever human beings congregate. Tellingly, most organizations – particularly post-financial crisis – have large teams devoted to the assessment of risk; we don't often hear of teams scanning the horizon for opportunity. This imbalance presents an opportunity for the optimist: it's a refreshing perspective that can gain easy traction, provided it is grounded in reality.

The kind of optimism we are talking about here is not delusional fantasy or 'irrational exuberance'. It's the ability to have an open mind to potential and possibility, without which progress is impossible. And 'rational optimism' is usually the product of encountering numerous obstacles in life and finding that, more often than not, solutions can be found.

A CEO told us:

'I have never subscribed to the ra-ra cheerleader approach to management. But at the same time you should never forget the role hope plays in motivating people. It is important that you can articulate why tomorrow will be better than today, that people feel they are on a development path that can take them to the next level. So the optimistic message is all about the "where"; it needs to be tempered with the pragmatic message that deals with the "how".'

AVOID TOXIC SELF-TALK

How do you respond to bad news or adverse criticism? We were struck, when working with one organization, to discover the range of interpretations different people would place on the same piece of feedback. One of the more senior managers with 20-odd years of experience was well known for marking up his juniors' documents with fairly pithy disparaging remarks such as: 'You can do better than this! Looks like a school essay – get to the point more quickly!'

Junior A remarked:

'I'm used to it. He doesn't have time to sugar-coat his feedback, and frankly I'm glad that he takes the trouble to read through what I do. He's busy, he makes his point, I take it on board and try to deliver what he wants next time.'

Contrast this with Junior B's response:

'He doesn't like me, that's the bottom line. He singles me out for this sort of dismissive stuff. It's a deliberate attempt to belittle me. I won't survive here long, that's pretty obvious.'

A range of possible interpretations is, of course, possible, but what would be your instinctive reflex? Do you tend to catastrophize – that is, put the worst possible interpretation on events? Or are you more measured, seeking clarification perhaps if you are unsure about the intention behind the criticism?

Toxic self-talk is sometimes the root of poor self-esteem. Influential people save their energy for battling genuine opponents rather than undermining themselves. What you tell yourself when you are on the receiving end of criticism or adversity is crucial – and to some extent determines an optimistic or pessimistic mindset. There are enough people out there who, given the chance, will do you down. Why join their number?

HELP OTHER PEOPLE SEE THE POSSIBILITIES AND POTENTIAL IN THEMSELVES

In the research for this book, we asked people we came into contact with about the individuals who had been most influential in their lives. We were expecting a huge variation in stories, given that we were talking to all ages, stages and cultures. In fact, there were two categories of 'influencer' that seemed to cross all of the boundaries: the teacher – who imparted wisdom or insight in a meaningful way – and the mentor, whose greatest gift seems to be in making the mentee aware of capabilities they didn't know they had.

The toxic self-talk we discussed above is, of course, not confined to you. It is endemic, particularly in high-achieving cultures or individuals. You can help others to be more optimistic about themselves without being too touchy-feely: just ask people to consider their range of options when talking disparagingly about themselves. For example:

- 'I'm going nowhere...' Really? Where would you like to be? What would be the first step towards getting there?
- 'I'm not good enough...' Is that true? Good enough for what? What would 'good' actually look like?

Helping other people to first recognize and then take steps towards achieving their potential is massively significant and – our research shows – rarely forgotten. Note that the intervention here is not intended to solve other people's problems or give them a palliative pat on the back; it is about helping them recognize they have options, the vital first step in combating 'learned helplessness'.

GATHER YOUR WAR STORIES

This is neither the time nor the place to debate whether people are born or made optimists. What is undoubtedly true, though, is that optimism can be worked on; the pessimistic reflex can, with practice, be resisted and reversed. Interestingly, one of the most powerful tools in assisting with this process is not some vague appeal to the power of positive thinking but a very specific cataloguing of your own track record in overcoming adversity.

The 'war story' is an account of how you successfully overcame difficulty or challenge in your life; what were the obstacles, what were the possible consequences, and how did you manage, against the odds, to prevail? We all have these stories; it's just that life moves on, and we forget about them. They contain tremendous power, however, for in these stories we find the rational basis for optimism – the groundwork that prevents the optimist being dismissed as an irrelevant fantasist.

Remind yourself of those times when you pulled it off despite the odds. Even better, when you are going through a period of adversity in your life, keep a diary. Record how despair over time turns to determination, darkness into light. Share these stories.

War stories are like gold dust in a presentation, and will often be the one thing that people respond to and remember.

An optimistic mindset is not the product of wishful thinking; it is the result of going through hell and coming out the other side. Optimism helps influence others because people are inspired by these stories – by the knowledge that they are not alone in their adversity, and that it can be overcome.

Putting it all together

Optimism is contagious. Project it, and your followers feel inspired. Connect it with your own freely shared life experience, and you come to be perceived as authentic, courageous and grounded. Show your followers that they have reason for optimism within themselves, and you can count on their support for life. Don't dismiss it; optimism is the prerequisite for progress.

- How do you speak to yourself? In particular, how harsh on yourself are you when you are criticized or when you fail? Can you introduce some balance?
- When did you last help someone identify their options? How attuned are you to other people's darker moods: despair, hopelessness or fear?
- Tell someone about a time in your life when you successfully overcame adversity. What lessons does that experience have for tough times still to come?

34 Master first impressions

'I've learned that people will forget what you said, people will forget what you did, but people will never forget how you made them feel.' Maya Angelou

'It takes 20 years to build a reputation and five minutes to ruin it. If you think about that, you'll do things differently.' Warren Buffett

'Don't reserve your best behaviour for special occasions. You can't have two sets of manners, two social codes – one for those you admire and want to impress, another for those whom you consider unimportant. You must be the same to all people.' Lillian Eichler Watson

'It is only shallow people who do not judge by appearances.' Oscar Wilde

Ian is a successful dealmaker with an unlikely recipe for success. A key part of his work in the private equity world is getting in sync with the owner-managers of family businesses. These businesses often go back generations, so there is a huge amount of emotional capital invested in them, and if Ian is going to persuade a family that his firm is the right one to partner with as the company looks to move to its next phase of development, he needs to build trust, and quickly.

'These people are often deeply suspicious of what they view as City types,' he explains. 'There is often some hostility in the room when we meet for the first time. Over the years, I've hit on a small thing that seems to make big difference. At the start of the meeting, after we have shaken hands and exchanged pleasantries, I will take my jacket off. Quite often I will roll up my shirtsleeves. The first time I did this, it was the middle of summer on a roasting day in a room with no air conditioning. But afterwards, the guy I was hoping to win over told me how powerful he found this simple gesture – he said he felt like I was communicating "I'm going to get down and dirty with this, I want to get straight to work." It was initially entirely coincidental, but I now use it consciously quite often. And others have said: "Hey, that thing you do with the jacket, it gives off the right sort of signals…"'

The research provides a range of answers for how long it takes someone to make a judgement of you based on a first impression, but the overall theme is pretty consistent: we're talking seconds rather than minutes. Get it wrong at the start and it's an uphill battle to stay in the conversation, let alone be influential.

Of course, this stuff only gets you so far: if you don't know what you are talking about, you are going to be exposed even if you made a great first impression. But too often we don't pay enough attention to the 'optics' of first interactions – and in doing so miss a trick in terms of positioning ourselves for success.

LOOK THE PART

Years ago I did some comparative analysis about first impressions with an accounting firm and its clients. What factors, I asked, were critically important in an initial interaction? The accountants' answers were predictable enough: subject-matter expertise, knowledge of industry, technical mastery. Imagine their surprise when they looked at the client responses: top of the list was 'quality attire'. I enquired around the room about the last time individuals had considered their wardrobe and invested in some new clothes for work. There were uncomfortable looks before most confessed that it was a subject they gave little thought to, and most would have been wearing the same business attire four years ago as they were wearing that day.

Whether we like it or not, people's impressions of us are guided in part by what we wear. This includes the quality, fit and colour of our clothes, but also whether we choose to fit in or stand out. For women, the choice – at least in theory – is much wider than for men. But do you exercise that choice? And how attuned are you to the dress codes of clients? Do you adjust what you wear according to circumstance, or is it a subject that just doesn't occur to you?

Be assured: even if you profess not to notice what other people wear, your colleagues and clients will be aware that you haven't bought a new suit in years.

AVOID THE SHAKE MISTAKE

Do you remember being on the receiving end of a hand crusher? What about a wet fish? The chances are that you formed an instant negative response in both cases, regardless of the conversation that followed. Indeed, Greg Stewart at the University of Iowa even conducted research into this area and concluded that, in job interviews at least, there was a correlation between a handshake perceived as 'mid-range' and being offered the job.

There seems to be particular potential for misinterpretation across gender lines. The following is typical of comments I hear in workshops from women discussing the impact certain male handshakes make on them:

'There's a certain type of guy who will shake your hand in a super-aggressive way, sort of turning your hand over so his is on top. I guess the point he's making is that he's not going to adapt his style because I am a woman, or maybe he thinks he's paying me a bizarre kind of compliment. Whatever, I loathe it, and form a negative impression of that person that's difficult to budge.'

There are, of course, cultural variations of the handshake, depending on what part of the world you are in. Are you aware of them?

Do you think about making eye contact at the point of shaking hands? It's a small thing, but one seasoned negotiator sets a lot of store by it:

'If I don't get eye contact during the handshake I always think that's defensive, and puts me in a one-up position. It's something I look out for.'

NURTURE THE GATEKEEPERS

The previous section concerns the first impressions we make with key stakeholders, but, of course, our interactions are also mediated by a host of others: secretaries, receptionists, assistants and deputies. We have an opportunity to make a great impression on the aides to the principal simply by acknowledging them, respecting them and passing the time of day if we have repeated interactions with them. To do otherwise invites disaster, as a CEO put it to me:

'I notice how people treat my staff, particularly junior or admin staff. There's a certain type of person that will not even acknowledge the person who brings them a coffee, or is short with the IT people when they are trying to set up their equipment in a pitch meeting. You can ooze all the charm you want to me, but if I sense that you switch it on and off according to perceived rank, you're not the sort of person I want to deal with.'

Quite apart from the impression it makes on the principal, getting the trust and respect of gatekeepers is sometimes the most effective way of gaining access and information. Rather than viewing them as an obstacle to be surmounted, next time work as hard on first impressions with the receptionist as with the CEO.

Putting it all together

Many of us think that it is the quality of our ideas that makes us influential, and that it is *intellectual* capital that really counts. The art of making a good first impression can seem trite or even trivial by comparison. Yet first impressions do count; and if making the most of them demands relatively little of you, why wouldn't you make that small investment?

- When did you last buy an item of clothing for work? How often do you review your wardrobe?
- Do you make yourself aware of cultural norms governing greetings in different parts of the world?
- How would you assess the strength of your relationship with the admin team at your biggest client?

35 Admit a weakness

> 'The whole problem with the world is that fools and fanatics are always so certain of themselves, but wiser men so full of doubts.' Bertrand Russell

> 'Acknowledging weakness doesn't make a leader less effective. On the contrary, in most cases it is simply a way of expressing that he understands what everyone else has known for some time. When you acknowledge your weaknesses to the rest of your team, it is never new information.' Andy Stanley

> 'I am careful not to confuse excellence with perfection. Excellence, I can reach for; perfection is God's business.' Michael J. Fox

> 'There must be something wrong with those people who think Audrey Hepburn doesn't perspire, hiccup or sneeze, because they know that's not true. In fact, I hiccup more than most.' Audrey Hepburn

> 'You grow up by making mistakes. I've made a ton of them, but as long as I keep on failing better, I don't mind.' Joely Richardson

In corporate life and elsewhere, the myth of Superman and Superwoman is still pervasive. We feel a need to conceal our flaws, juggle the impossible and consider perfection as the only reasonable standard by which we may be judged. When ugly reality intrudes – in the form of mistakes, bad luck or routine failure – we go into damage limitation mode, spinning events to ensure that, if blame gets bandied around, it won't be sticking to us.

In this, we are mirroring what we see in public life. Admitting a mistake, an error of judgement or a personal weakness is still considered fatal in politics, for instance. When did you last hear a politician admit he got it wrong? And years after the great financial crisis, many of the major players are still citing extenuating circumstances for the disaster rather than admitting weakness or responsibility themselves. Even Lance Armstrong, whose self-inflicted fall from grace was pretty stupendous, found it difficult to take full responsibility and apologize for his actions in his famous Oprah interview. Most public figures appear in denial about weaknesses that are all too obvious to everyone else; the famous Frost/Nixon encounter offers another celebrated example.

This obsession with appearing flawless is entirely counterproductive. No one is perfect, so anyone appearing to manufacture the illusion of it arouses deep distrust, often hostility. It is precisely because of this phenomenon that the admission of weakness is such a powerful tactic in increasing trust and influence. Honesty about one's shortcomings as well as one's strengths is so unusual that it makes you stand out from the crowd as being, perhaps, better balanced and more 'human' than most.

It needs careful handling, though: being too honest about oneself too much of the time can be damaging. Acknowledging a weakness in an area absolutely fundamental to performance should also be avoided. Not many of us would sit easily in our seats following a pilot's announcement at the start of a flight to the effect that he's never been good with heights.

Nevertheless, the selective and honest admission of the odd personal foible can often be interpreted as a sign of integrity and strength. It is just a matter of picking the right time and the right tone.

APOLOGIZE

To err is human, we are told, but how often do we put our hand up and acknowledge our own error? Of course, there are occasions when an apology may be construed as an admission of liability, with all the implications that entails – and these are the times when saying nothing makes sense while we consult our legal advisers.

However, most of the time the stakes are not that high: we just screw up, plain and simple. Why not say so, without hesitation or reservation?

The gold standard for apology in the corporate world was set by the budget airline JetBlue. In 2007, a snowstorm and its impact on the airline left several thousand passengers inconvenienced for many hours. The CEO David Neeleman sent a letter to each passenger, which began:

'We are sorry and embarrassed. But most of all we are deeply sorry.'

He went on to outline the steps the company would take to prevent a recurrence of the delays. But what people appreciated was the tone; we are so used to apologies, particularly, corporate ones, being defensive and partial that the simplicity and honesty were refreshing.

RECOGNIZE YOUR SHORTCOMINGS, AND KEEP WORKING ON THEM

The critical point in the life of many entrepreneurs is when they realize they can't do it all. They have strengths, often amazing ones, but they have areas of weakness, too. And at that point they either need to hire other people whose skillsets complement their own, or do some serious personal development.

The same applies in everyday life, whether or not you are trying to grow a business. Being able to identify and articulate your own weaknesses, and appreciate the complementary strengths of other people, shows a level of emotional maturity not apparent in everyone. And while this kind of honesty is usually appreciated, for it to become inspiring, you need to show that awareness of weakness is just the first phase. The next is evidence that you are 'working' on your weaknesses, that continuous personal development is something you take seriously.

The best answer to the hoary old interview question 'What's your biggest weakness?' therefore is not 'perfectionism' or some other contrivance designed to offer a weakness that isn't really a weakness. The best answer is to be honest: 'X is my biggest weakness.' And then offer a plan: 'Here's what I'm doing about it…'

BE OPEN TO CRITICAL FEEDBACK

All this assumes that we are familiar with our own weaknesses, whereas often they need to be brought to our attention by other people. To be genuinely receptive to critical feedback, to establish a culture where such feedback is not only permissible but welcomed, requires guts, but it may enable you to pick up insights about yourself that make a crucial difference to your performance. If you are serious about it, you may need to establish a mechanism whereby people can comment anonymously – giving critical feedback face to face can feel uncomfortable, especially if you are more senior than the person offering the feedback.

Putting it all together

Vulnerability doesn't have many friends at the moment. Everywhere we look, in fields from religion to politics, as well as in the corporate world and often in our personal life, black and white seem more potent than myriad shades of grey. Perhaps that is why this technique has such power – it is the minor chord that puts the rest of the melody into relief. Try it: reveal a weakness. Acknowledge a flaw. See how the world responds.

- When did you last apologize, unreservedly and publicly?
- What is your biggest weakness, and how open are you about it?
- Where do you go for critical feedback?

36 'Yes, and...'

'If you don't have the smoking gun, then it's pointless to hector interviewees. Because you just shut people up instead of opening them up. I always used to quote the old Aesop fable about the sun and the wind having a competition to get someone's coat off. That is the key to drawing people out and also developing a sense of trust.' Sir David Frost

Everything has beauty, but not everyone sees it.' Confucius

'The really good idea is always traceable back quite a long way, often to a not very good idea which sparked off another idea that was only slightly better, which somebody else misunderstood in such a way that they then said something which was really rather interesting.' John Cleese

'Be the one who nurtures and builds. Be the one who has an understanding and a forgiving heart, the one who looks for the best in people. Leave people better than you found them.' Marvin J. Ashton

'Is constructive criticism really constructive? Not really. You can't make a child better by pointing out what you think is wrong with him or her. Criticism either crushes spirit or elicits defensiveness. Constructive criticism is an interesting combination of words. "Construct" means "to build". "Criticism" means "to tear down". It creates defiance and anger as well.' H. Norman Wright

Sadly, I think the urge to destroy is probably innate in humans. I came to this dispiriting conclusion in the way many of us do: by watching my young children at play. For example, no matter how carefully I constructed a sandcastle with my daughter – however meticulous I was in the ordering of seashells and seaweed, however delighted she seemed by the moat and the ramparts and the lolly stick flag on the top – the real glint in her eye came right at the end as she prepared to smash the whole edifice into smithereens. It's the same story with those little blocks you make towers out of, or play dough, or clay. Young children will humour you during the construction phase, but will get their real kick out of stomping your creation into dust.

I don't think the destructive urge ever really leaves us. Look at Twitter: it is seething with 'trolls'. I follow one or two sports pundits – people who have played to a professional standard and whose views deserve to be respected. Occasionally, I notice people ask their opinions about a player or a match situation, and, to their credit, these pundits sometimes reply with an honest view or two. You might think that the person who posed the initial question might then have the decency to thank the ex-pros for their view and disappear stage right. Not a bit of it: they usually come back and contest the answer, rubbish the opinion, challenge the pundit to a fight and call him every name under the sun. This is the online equivalent of the child kicking over the sandcastle in a quiet corner of the beach, except that the protagonist is presumably an adult and the arena a completely public one.

Somewhere along the line, Descartes' famous maxim has become distorted: it has become I *disagree*, therefore I am.

What if, rather than seeking instinctively to challenge and destroy another's idea, we train ourselves to assume merit unless conclusively proved otherwise?

'YES, AND…' VS. 'AH, BUT…'

There's nothing wrong with a critical mind except when it only has one note. If the *default* response in your team or firm to any new idea or thought or opinion is to find its flaws and shoot it down, the consequence is inevitable: a climate of fear, seething resentment and the premature death of a thousand great ideas.

Often in workshops, when I outline a new piece of academic research or an item in the news that has interested me, I will notice eyes narrowing and brows crinkling. Pretty soon, the hands will start to go up and people will say things starting with phrases like:

- 'Don't you think that…?'
- 'There's an inconsistency here…'
- 'I'm not sure that this applies in my world…'

Before they can possibly have fully understood the point I am making, the default response is to disagree, to criticize or even to ridicule.

What if the next time someone volunteers an opinion and you have something to add, you try doing it in the spirit of accretion rather than demolition? This means that you take the initial idea as a foundation and attempt to build on it to test its firmness, rather than wanting to rip it up for the sake of it, with nothing to put in its place.

ACCENTUATE THE POSITIVE

One of the most common complaints we hear about life in organizations big or small is that, while the mistakes are seized upon, the good stuff goes unnoticed. Maybe this mindset was entirely appropriate in an earlier era of industrialization and vast manufacturing enterprises, where a mistake could often have life-or-death consequences. But the majority of us now do not work on oil rigs or in coalmines. The threat of death in the workplace has receded.

The genuinely influential leader will be one who realizes that better productivity in a knowledge-based organization is all about helping new ideas develop and thrive. And that requires not only a revision of the 'Ah, but…' mentality but also a willingness to look out for and comment on the good work people do. There is a lot of talk about developing a 'culture of innovation' but rarely an equivalent commitment to creating a culture of confidence, where people feel empowered to innovate and improve because they know their contribution will be noticed and valued.

We asked many of our interviewees to recall a boss they found particularly influential, and the following is a typical response:

'The only boss I ever respected in my entire career was a guy who would dispense with the formal part of the annual appraisal in about five minutes and spend the rest of the hour identifying what he thought I had excelled at and trying to find ways in which I could do more of that stuff. I found that inspiring, and I've tried to do the same. I don't wait for the annual appraisal with my team, though; I try to have those conversations every couple of months.'

EXPRESS BENIGN CURIOSITY

If your work requires you to elicit information from other people – and, even if it is not part of the formal job description, this will be a task few of us can avoid completely – a look at the contrasting styles of two celebrated TV interviewers might prove instructive.

In the UK, the doyens of the political interview are the late David Frost and Jeremy Paxman. Their styles could not be further apart. Paxman starts his interviews as antagonist-in-chief: he makes clear his disdain for the hapless interviewee, and proceeds to prod and poke the unfortunate victim in the manner of a farmer dealing with his errant sheep.

Frost, by contrast, came across as the interviewee's slightly befuddled confidant. There was the air of a relaxed gentleman's club about his interviews.

Paxman is most famous for his grilling of a Tory Home Secretary, Michael Howard. He asked Howard the same question, with increasing exasperation, a total of 12 times. Paxman fans often forget that, even at the twelfth time of asking, he failed to elicit an answer.

Frost, by contrast, with his perennial attitude of benign curiosity, charmed the truth out of most people.

A confrontational attitude produces confrontation. Curiosity often elicits the truth.

The 'Yes, and ...' stance is at the heart of a collaborative approach to everyday interaction, but we see it all too rarely. Ego gets in the way, and to agree with someone or to help develop their idea can feel like a surrendering of the initiative, a ceding of ground.

It's not how it works in many creative fields, however, where collaboration is at the heart of success. Lennon and McCartney were famous for providing a finishing touch to the other's work. If their instinct had been to destroy each other's creativity rather than add to it, we would never have got to hear songs like 'We Can Work It Out' or 'Day in the Life'.

- Do you tend to look for the flaws or the possibilities in new ideas?
- When did you last give someone positive feedback on something they did particularly well?
- How effective are you at getting people to disclose what they are truly thinking and feeling?

37 Work on emotional intelligence

❝ 'There is no separation of mind and emotions; emotions, thinking and learning are all linked.' Eric Jensen

❝ 'What really matters for success, character, happiness and life-long achievements is a definite set of emotional skills – your EQ – not just purely cognitive abilities that are measured by conventional IQ tests.' Daniel Goleman

❝ 'Use pain as a stepping stone, not a camp ground.' Alan Cohen

❝ 'Beginning today, treat everyone you meet as if they were going to be dead by midnight. Extend them all the care, kindness and understanding you can muster. Your life will never be the same again.' Og Mandino

❝ 'He who smiles rather than rages is always the stronger.' Japanese proverb

Daniel Goleman published *Emotional Intelligence: Why It Can Matter More Than IQ* way back in 1995, and in the two decades since then the term has gone on to achieve worldwide prominence. However, rather like other buzz phrases – think of 'global warming' or 'quantitative easing' – this one is more bandied about than fully understood. And even those who profess to understand the phrase seem reluctant to practise it.

In our workshops with new entrants to the professions – 'Generation Y', in effect – we sometimes set exercises on the subject of persuasion and influence and ask the delegates to tell us how they will go about, for example, asking their manager for more interesting and varied work. Their typical response will be to use 'good for me' and 'assertiveness' tactics. The first will frame the conversation in terms of entitlement: 'It is my right to be granted interesting work opportunities; it is therefore beholden on you, my manager, to hear my plea and action it immediately if you want to keep me happy.' When we suggest that this approach may not be met with immediate agreement, they tend to resort to a sort of shrill repetition: 'It's my right... If you don't give me what I want, I'll need to reconsider my future here' and, ultimately, 'It's not fair...'

Only seeing things your way and attempting to persuade others by force or emotional blackmail are not tactics you will find in the pages of Goleman's book. In fact, they are an inversion of emotional intelligence, where the key attributes seem to be an ability to understand the other side's point of view and a willingness to express oneself respectfully and with tact.

Perhaps the effort required of emotional intelligence does not fit our time-poor age. It seems like too much bother to understand someone else's point of view; it is far quicker to batter them with our own self-righteousness and hope that they fall like long grass beneath a scythe.

This is to use influence like a blunt instrument – it will sometimes miss the target and often cause more damage than intended. Emotional intelligence – particularly when you are influencing across generations or across cultures – offers a more sophisticated tool, and one that can deliver results that stick.

SEE IT FROM THEIR SIDE

The most powerful question you can ask when trying to influence someone is 'What's in it for them?' When coercion is neither possible nor desirable – you have no line authority, for example – aiming for the win–win is the only way you are going to get any traction.

Does what you are proposing make the other person's life easier or more difficult? If it is the former, make sure that you communicate this clearly. If it is the latter, what can you do to show due consideration and perhaps make things better? Rather than presenting someone with a problem, present them with a solution, or at least the beginnings of one.

Emily, a law firm partner, shares this example:

'Associates often come and ask to go on secondment to a client or another office. The occasions when I am minded to give their request some consideration is when they have clearly done a bit of homework and looked at it from my side. They appreciate the resourcing difficulties, they will have considered briefing a replacement, and they will come with client relationships of mine that stand to gain from the arrangement. But most of the time they say, "I'd like to go on secondment because it would be really great for my career." Those conversations are not the productive ones!'

So a bit of forethought and planning is important, but it is dangerous to make too many assumptions about what someone will think about a subject. Enter these conversations with genuine curiosity. 'I know what I think on this – how about you? What's your perspective?'

MASTER YOUR OWN EMOTIONS

Again and again, interviewees for this book mentioned calmness as a key to influence. If you can impress in a crisis, if you can 'keep your head when all about you are losing theirs', this seems to be among the most important things you can do to garner respect and be taken seriously.

An army officer with responsibility for preparing soldiers for conflict draws this distinction:

'You notice that, in times of crisis, there are people who fall victim to their emotions – and that's excitement and adrenaline-rush as well as fear – and those who don't. That's not to say that this latter camp aren't feeling the same levels of stress; it's just that they have worked out a way to stop it interfering with their communication and their decision-making process. They can detach themselves emotionally from the situation. Later, of course, they will find a way of releasing that tension, but in some people crisis brings out the best and in others it brings out the worst.'

This is not, of course, to advocate some kind of bloodless, robotic approach to life. The key point the officer makes is that the emotion is still present; it just doesn't impair one's ability to operate.

Does a display of emotion – anger, conviction or disagreement – enhance the message or detract from it? Is it immediately apparent what your mood is, how high your level of stress?

A veteran of numerous buy-outs, a private equity specialist reflects on the use of emotion in negotiation:

'You do see it used as a tactic sometimes, the bloke who goes ballistic, throwing his toys out of the pram. My view is that it is entirely counterproductive. It makes the other side really dig in. What really impresses is someone in control of their own emotions and also acutely aware of other people's.'

EXPECT DIFFERENCE

What are the general rules for emotional intelligence, then? There's probably only one, and it is beloved of NLP practitioners everywhere: remember that the map is not the territory. Expecting everyone else, in negotiations or important meetings, to have the same priorities as you or to respond the same way to circumstances is asking for trouble. The best influencers in these situations simply make no assumptions, but make it their business to find out the other side's view through careful and patient questioning and observation. Assuming difference rather than similarity, and being motivated to better understand it, transforms the effectiveness of your interactions.

'It's very in vogue to talk about difference in gender terms or cultural terms,' a leader in the UK public sector told us. 'But I think it's broader than that. I became much more effective when I started to realize how many assumptions I made about people I didn't even know. Now, when I'm negotiating or attempting to influence, I spend twice the time attempting to really understand the other side's drivers as I do expressing my own. I take nothing for granted. I'm a guy with 20 years' senior-level management experience, but I try to stop looking at everyone and everything through that lens. And when it comes to my turn to put my point of view, I try to be completely honest, which often means dispensing with the professional persona of invincibility. I say, "This is really important to me..." or "We have a difference of opinion here..." or "I haven't fully worked this out yet..." Emotional honesty I call it, as opposed to emotional intelligence...'

'The map is not the territory.'

Putting it all together

How well do you read other people? Do you find yourself quick to judge, putting people into boxes of 'like me' or 'unlike me' and not bothering to explore any further? Or do you withhold judgement – seeking to understand others with the influencer's most potent weapons, questioning and listening?

The key to emotional intelligence is not deference or assertiveness but a determination to see the other side's point of view with the same clarity you see your own. It is time-consuming and occasionally puts you in a position of vulnerability; but ultimately makes for agreements, and relationships, that stand the test of time.

- When you want something from someone, do you think through the benefits for them?
- How apparent is your mood to outside observers? Can you control your emotions, particularly under stress?
- How often do you make assumptions about beliefs and behaviours? When did you last approach a conversation with an attitude of genuine curiosity?

38 Reinvent yourself periodically

 ❝ 'When things are bad, it's the best time to reinvent yourself.'
George Lopez

 ❝ 'Write down ten things you would do in your life if you had absolutely no fear. Then pick one of them and do it.' **Steve Chandler**

 ❝ 'If you're going to stick around in this business, you have to have the ability to reinvent yourself, whether consciously or unconsciously.' **Dennis Quaid**

 ❝ 'There is nothing noble about being superior to some other man. The nobility is in being superior to your previous self.'
Hindu proverb

'Avoid typecasting' is one of the key lessons drummed into trainee actors. No matter how tempting it might be to coast along in your predictable niche, churning out the same type of performance over and over again, in the end it is entirely self-defeating. The parts dry up, staleness creeps in and suddenly you are yesterday's man.

It's instructive to look at the career of Sir Ian McKellen to see how a very conscious strategy to evade typecasting has paid off handsomely. McKellen built his reputation in the theatre and came to be regarded as one of the great classical actors of his generation. His Macbeth in 1976 is still remembered as one of the definitive portrayals; by his mid-40s he had conquered most of the great stage roles, and could easily have carried on for the rest of his career reprising his earlier successes and doing one-man shows to (relatively) small but ecstatically appreciative audience of theatre-goers.

Instead, he made a conscious effort to reinvent himself as a film actor – and one, moreover, who would play a quite startling array of parts. From Magneto in *X-Men* to Gandalf in *Lord of the Rings*, as he moved into his 60s he was demonstrating a versatility that brought him the acclaim of new audiences barely a third of his age.

Reinvention is also the hallmark of longevity in the field of popular music. Most artists who manage to stay in vogue long after their contemporaries have faded from view tend to be masters at manipulating their public image. The classic example would, of course, be Bob Dylan, who has forged a 50-year career in the public eye by morphing from beatnik folkie to gnarled bluesman via spells as country music crooner and born-again Christian.

What seems common practice in the arts world – the need to keep changing, keep innovating – rarely seems to translate to the world of business. Yet staleness is the enemy of all careers, not just those in the public eye. Longevity in and of itself is often the key to influence, and strategic reinvention is one of the best ways of achieving it.

RETOOL CONSTANTLY

For the vast majority of us, the process of formal learning is over by the age of 21 at the latest. We mostly rely on the skills and insight gained at a very early stage of life to see us through the next three or four decades or more. 'Lifelong learning' is a quaint term that has come to mean a little mid-life dabbling with a foreign language, perhaps, but nothing at all to do with the mainstream business of our lives.

This is a mistake. Adding emerging skills to your portfolio, or keeping existing ones refreshed, is critical to your longevity. So how seriously do you take it? What are the ways in which you keep your ears open for new developments in your field? How many days a year do you devote to your own professional reinvigoration?

People who manage this successfully seem to blend formal means of learning – training courses, university programmes and the like – with less formal options. A respected entrepreneur told us:

'I always make a point of buying magazines I wouldn't normally read if I'm passing through an airport, or listening to radio programmes while I'm driving that I would probably otherwise ignore. Just occasionally you'll hear of stuff going on in other fields that has a resonance in your own... There are always new ideas, new approaches that can help you take your own practice forwards.'

HAVE MORE THAN ONE STRING

We live in an age where second and third careers are common, and often these take the form of a hobby that became a profession. Developing a passion completely unrelated to your principal job of work can be a useful insurance policy for later life, but can also add lustre to your office profile, too. A friend's landscape photography was so admired by his work colleagues that he was asked by the senior management to provide the imagery for the firm's annual report. His work was put on show in the organization's head office, prompting further orders from clients and colleagues. He became known across the business as 'the guy who takes those great photos', prompting questions and interactions from colleagues he would never normally meet. Eventually, an unexpected but highly profitable second career began to emerge.

Cultivate your extracurricular interests, but bring them into school sometimes, too...

PUT YOUR HAND UP

People are always looking for volunteers to help scope out a new initiative. Steering groups, committees and discussion groups are all natural habitats of early adopters, but the rest of us tend to to avoid joining such groups, if at all possible. However, we should realize that they offer us an opportunity to meet different people, get associated with new initiatives and perhaps exceed or extend our usual brief. And if you agree with Woody Allen that much of our success in life comes down to just showing up, then there is almost certainly an advantage to be gained by being one of the few to actively engage in these types of discussions.

The next time an email comes around asking for assistance, or feedback, or a point of view, or a willingness to put in a couple of hours discussing something, why not say yes rather than hitting delete? Doing the stuff other people can't be bothered to do is an effective – though gruelling – path to influence. Showing up on a Thursday night when most of your colleagues have given in to the temptation of a glass of red wine at home can pay dividends, as one of our banking clients relates:

'I did turn up once at a meeting to look at emerging markets. There were a couple of senior managers there, a VP and me. And they were going through all the various markets we should be putting more energy into. And, at the end, they asked for volunteers to do more research into various places and I put my hand up for Turkey, largely because I'd been there on holiday! And because of that, I started to get invited to conferences on Turkey, and became known as the go-to guy for Turkey and it took my career on a different path. All because I tuned up at this meeting when 99 per cent of my colleagues couldn't be bothered…'

Putting it all together

It's usually only in retrospect that we realize that the niche we thought we'd comfortably cornered for life actually had a sell-by date all along. Inertia, habit and the pull of the comfort zone are hard to resist. Those who remain influential over a long period of time are alive to this danger, and are adept at ensuring that they embrace and facilitate change rather than being a victim of it. A willingness to keep learning and a desire to bring all their talents into play, however apparently incompatible, are valuable strengths here.

It takes courage to evade stereotyping and continue to demonstrate versatility and a willingness to try new things, particularly later in life. The first step is to realize the onset of staleness before anyone else does. When did you last learn something new? When were you last discomfited by the size of the challenge in the day ahead? When did you last put your hand up and suggest a new approach, a new role for yourself, a change of direction?

If the answer to these questions is 'not recently', the time for action is now. Start drawing up new plans for tomorrow before you become yesterday's news.

- Are you pigeonholed?
- What is your 'second string'?
- What opportunities exist to demonstrate your versatility?

Part 5

How you play the game:
influence through politics

Associate with the influential

> 'Our chief want in life is somebody who will make us do what we can.' Ralph Waldo Emerson

> 'My mentor said, "Let's do it", not "You go do it". How powerful when someone says "Let's…"' Brian Tracy

> 'If you want to be successful, find someone who has achieved the results you want and copy what they do and you'll achieve the same results.' Anthony Robbins

> 'Women have twice as many mentors as men, but half as many sponsors. Sponsors advocate on [behalf of] their protégé, connecting them to important players and assignments. In doing so, they make themselves look good.' Ann Hewlett

Influence is contagious. Just as proximity to a heat source guarantees us a certain amount of warmth, so affiliating ourselves with the genuinely influential means that we bask in their reflected glory. We are able to access their insight, their experience and their network, and other people's perception of us changes once we are known to be part of the 'inner circle'. Influence, in part, comes down to the company we choose to keep.

The opposite is also true. It's very difficult to be influential when we don't have either positional authority (rank, title, prestige) or the ear of those who do.

How do we build these relationships with integrity, then, without resorting to sycophancy or unsavoury politics? The first step is to identify the real sources of power – or potential power – within your organization. Don't confuse power with popularity; corporate and political life is littered with the corpses of perfectly able lieutenants whose captains never made it to general. They nailed their colours to the wrong mast. It is natural that we gravitate towards those personalities we feel more comfortable with; the trouble is that congeniality is no indicator of influence. Once we have a sense of who really wields the power, we can begin to assess our own relationships with those people and perhaps consider how we can get a little closer.

At first glance, there may appear to be little we can offer those in authority – we may shy away from developing top-level relationships for fear of seeming needy, calculating or impertinent. This is to underestimate the isolating effect of power. The higher one rises in a hierarchy, the greater the danger of disconnect with the masses. This could be where you come in. While you stand to gain plenty from associating with the influential, it is not a one-way street. You have plenty to offer in return.

BE A SOUNDING BOARD

One of the most frequent complaints made by those who have climbed to the top of the career ladder is that it gets ever more difficult to gain perspective on their situation. They are surrounded by people who will be directly affected by their key decisions, so they carry with them their own self-interested agendas. If you offer an outside perspective, and can demonstrate complete trustworthiness, you may be surprised at the access you can get to top-level decision makers.

Roland was an accountant whose firm specialized in working with entrepreneurs looking to fund or start up new businesses. He found himself at an early stage of his career in meetings with a well-known entrepreneur.

'I was intimidated at first, as I'd seen him a few times on TV. But the odd thing was, even though I was the most junior person by a long way at those meetings, he would often ask for my input.

And I must have made some sort of impact because he would then phone me up occasionally and just ramble away about what was going on, even talk me through deals that I had no real knowledge of. He would do 90 per cent of the talking and then at the end would say "Thanks, that's been really helpful," even though I'd contributed next to nothing.'

Sometimes it's not insight or experience you can offer a senior player; it is simply objectivity and a willingness to listen.

BE THEIR EYES AND EARS

Knowledge is power, but the higher up one goes in a hierarchy the more difficult it can become to hear the unvarnished truth about what people are thinking and feeling. If you are in a position to communicate such information to those in authority, your value will rise. Of course, this has its unscrupulous aspect. We can all think of people who trade on gossip and badmouthing others, and whose motive is primarily self-serving. But if your motive is benign, sharing your own, radically different, perspective can be a smart strategy.

Kerry worked in a large call centre that was experiencing an unusually high level of 'churn'. Management put out a questionnaire, which few employees responded to, and began investigating different remuneration packages.

'I knew what was putting a lot of people off. There was one supervisor who was viewed as a bit of a bully, and even though she only had about 20 direct reports, there was a bad vibe on that floor because of her. And the other thing, which was really silly in a way, was that people were bored with the canteen food. It hadn't changed in the two years I'd been here, and because we're right out in the middle of nowhere, people didn't have any options. So, rather than fill in this questionnaire, I just asked to see the manager and made these points direct. The food is still not brilliant but it's better, the supervisor seems to have chilled out, and I get asked from time to time to go in and talk to management about what's happening on the floor. I prefer to do something about stuff like that than sit around and whinge.'

HELP WITH THEIR LEGACY

There comes a point in every successful person's life when they start thinking about their legacy: what lasting impression will they have made on their team, their business and the wider world? This is usually the time when they have a real urge to 'put something back'. There might be an increase in charity work, or the acceptance of invitations to boards and committees that they have hitherto shunned. Why not add another task to their altruistic list: sponsoring you and your career?

If you are young enough not to be a threat to their position, but have genuine promise, there is every chance key influencers will consider that engaging with you to build your potential and your profile is time well worth spending. After all, every successful person needs a protégé.

How do you make this happen? Pluck up the courage and ask. Many organizations spend thousands on mentoring and coaching schemes, where individuals are paired up with well-meaning advisers who sit and listen to them moan. No wonder the return on investment is difficult to measure. It is far better instead to get the active sponsorship of someone who knows where the bodies are hidden, and has the political clout to fast-track your career.

Putting it all together

Alas, the 'in crowd' doesn't just exist at high school. It is a feature of life wherever people gather and work together. Certain groupings are more influential than others, and influence tends to congregate around the top brass and rising stars. You need to be part of that crowd, because influence grows by association.

There are a variety of legitimate currencies you can trade in order to be of value to those more powerful than you: for example, objectivity, intelligence and appealing to their need to 'give something back'.

A couple of words of warning need to be stated around this tactic. Be careful not to trade too publicly on your association with the powerful – you can end up alienating both your sponsor and your rivals. Discretion is key. And make sure that, if you have been the beneficiary of a mentoring or sponsorship arrangement, you reciprocate when you achieve a position of power or influence yourself. 'Pulling the ladder up' behind you once you have got to the top is a sure-fire recipe for animosity, resentment and the gradual erosion of your hard-won influence.

- Who are the key influencers in your organization?
- Can you help secure their legacy?
- Can you listen to them without needing to pass judgement?

40 Keep your distance

> **''** 'One sees qualities at a distance and defects at close range.'
> Victor Hugo

> **''** 'Life is like a landscape. You live in the midst of it but can describe it only from the vantage point of distance.'
> Charles Lindbergh

> **''** 'Every man is surrounded by a neighbourhood of voluntary spies.' Jane Austen

> **''** 'Stay away from people who gossip and spread rumours. They are choosing the path of emotional bullying and negativity.'
> Steve Maraboli

> **''** 'Dispassionate objectivity is itself a passion, for the real and for the truth.' Abraham Maslow

At some juncture in your career, you will need to choose between popularity and respect. This is a transition that eludes many, because the personal cost to friendships and conviviality is too great. Yet influence accrues to those who are able to make the tough calls, particularly those that involve other people's careers and livelihoods. If you are one of those people who like to be part of a crowd, particularly a crowd of peers, your decision-making may be compromised by familiarity.

In many of the interviews for this book, people were at pains to point out that their influence was hard won. There is a price to be paid in the pursuit of high achievement and it seems to take a particularly heavy toll on peer-level relationships. There comes a point where you will need to tell someone that their performance isn't good enough; that their pet project is going to be aborted; that they have missed out on promotion. At these moments, can you make the call between what is right and what is comfortable?

It is all made a lot easier if you get into the habit of putting a little distance between yourself and your team members as you rise up the ranks. Sport, once again, provides us with some useful examples: a coach's effectiveness is severely compromised if he cannot stop thinking of himself as 'one of the boys'.

A football coach told us:

'I came up through the youth system with a lot of the lads I now manage. That's not been easy. In the early days I would go and have a beer with them exactly like old times. But then you need to take tough decisions and you find your judgement gets clouded, and people start trying to influence you, and in the end it was just easier to stop having the drinks. I built my social life well away from football. It was a shame, but I needed to be able to make decisions without emotion getting in the way.'

It's not just the tough calls. Creativity and freshness are difficult to achieve in an atmosphere that has grown too familiar.

A little distance – between people and places – can be good news.

AVOID GOSSIP

There's something seductive about gossip. It bonds people around the water cooler and provides the content for so much barroom chat. The notion of being on the inside track, of being in possession of classified information, is a thrill that's hard to resist.

You must.

Participating in gossip is about the drawing of invisible lines. You become complicit with your co-gossipers. This will limit your freedom of action, even if you regard yourself as peripheral and not the instigator of these types of conversations. When the object of the gossip gets to hear about it, you will still become persona non grata. And, perhaps more insidiously, your joining in will be treated as tacit approval by your co-gossipers. You are 'one of them'. How does that feel?

It is far better to operate on the principle that you only say things in private that you are happy to stand by in public. Many employment tribunals might have been avoided that way. Gossip impacts on your integrity and your freedom to make decisions: leave it to others and ask, politely, to be excused.

DON'T NAIL YOUR COLOURS TO ONLY ONE MAST

Just as guilt by association is a real possibility with idle gossip, the same is also true with your senior-level relationships. Many influential careers have floundered when close association with the 'coming man' didn't survive his eventual ousting. There's nothing wrong with having an influential mentor – indeed, it has been discussed as a success strategy earlier in the book – but the smart influencer will ensure that his or her top-level contacts are spread about a bit. You don't want to lose everything placing a bet on the wrong horse.

Amanda was a campaign co-ordinator for a political party.

'I was quite close to a senior party figure. He was the reason I got into politics, so obviously the chance to work closely with him was fantastic. I became associated with him in other people's eyes, and that gave me amazing levels of access when he was in his prime. The trouble was, he was on his way out when I got to know him and he left politics after a couple of years. The new guy looked at me as being part of the old regime, and, although there was no animosity between the two of them at the top, he got rid of me and put his own people in my place. That's politics.'

It is indeed politics, and not just in political parties. Even the most enlightened leader may see things in a starkly binary way: 'If you are not with me, you're against me.'

Unless you are absolutely certain that your mentor is in an unassailable position, you may want to play this by avoiding too public a declaration of support. Give tacit support instead: pledge full allegiance in private, but avoid a public declaration until it is unavoidable. Keep your options open.

GET SOME PERSPECTIVE

Have you ever found that it's easier to see a solution to someone else's problems than it is to find one for your own? Researchers at Cornell University actually discovered this to be a verifiable phenomenon: familiarity actually hinders problem solving.[1] The more familiar you are with a situation, its actors and its context, the more difficult you are going to find it to make creative suggestions, come up with solutions and generally see the wood for the trees. This is why trainees and new starters in an organization can acquire a position of influence quite quickly: they have the advantage of fresh perspective. They see things that are obvious, but not to the stale eye.

You need to take steps to ensure that your appreciation of a situation is not dulled through proximity. Your options for gaining perspective are plentiful:

- Have a trusted mentor completely outside your team or organization.
- Set up an informal group of peers from across your industry but outside your firm.
- Take a sabbatical.
- Ask for a secondment, where appropriate.
- Work from home one day a week.
- Take an evening class.

Gaining perspective can perhaps even involve simply taking a walk in the park this lunchtime rather than listening to the everyday moans and whinges of your colleagues in the coffee shop.

Here is our football coach again:

'Every so often I will practise somewhere different. We'll go to a park or a school. It's interesting that when you put people in a new situation they see new patterns of play, new possibilities that they would never have seen at our training ground. There it's predictable, and I want to get them away from that.'

---

1 'Decisions for Others Are More Creative Than Decisions for the Self', *Personality and Social Psychology Bulletin* 37/4 (Apr 2011): 492–501

Familiarity breeds contempt, as the saying has it. We need to be watchful of the corrosive effects of proximity – to power, to people and to places. We can retain our neutrality by avoiding the trap of colluding with indiscreet gossip; our flexibility by refusing to publicly endorse the claims of those more senior than us on the rise; and our creativity by seeking an escape from the claustrophobia of an environment we know too well. The dangerous aspect of all these threats is that they creep up on us unnoticed over time. If we are not careful, we find our colours nailed to the wrong mast without the time to change them.

- Would you describe yourself as someone who enjoys gossip?
- Do you have a mentor or a senior champion? How secure is their position within the hierarchy? How public is your support for them?
- How do you get perspective on your team, organization or workplace?

41 Show ruthlessness – but sparingly

> 'This is a ruthless world and one must be ruthless to cope with it.' Charlie Chaplin

> 'Is self-interest a bad thing? We want our leaders to be pure and good, but at the same time we want them to be effective, and to be effective you often have to be ruthless and not bound by ideology or the same morals that we pretend to hold ourselves to.' Beau Willimon

> 'The supreme art of war is to subdue the enemy without fighting.' Sun Tzu

> 'When men cut jobs, they're seen as decisive. When women do, they're vindictive.' Carly Fiorina

> 'People say I am ruthless. I am not ruthless. And if I find the man who is calling me ruthless, I shall destroy him.' Robert Kennedy

There are two fundamental archetypes for the influencer. On the one hand sits the sage, who achieves his influential position thanks to the strength of his intellect, insight or vision. He seems to see the world in a different way from other people, and it is in the communication of his unique perspective that he gains his strength. On the other sits – or rather stands – the samurai, who owes his eminence to his ruthless pursuit of power. His influence derives from courage and self-belief, an inner sense that he has what it takes to command and to lead, and he bears the scars for all to see of battles won and opponents slayed in the furtherance of that aim.

Like all such dichotomies, it is misleading. Knowledge without power is a recipe for frustration; power without knowledge often a recipe for disaster.

Sometimes, in order to be truly influential, an individual cannot rely on the softer skills of persuasion and consensus-building alone. Sometimes, he will have to wield the knife. An examination of any major politician's career will usually reveal one such moment of ruthlessness, which, in effect, enables the influence that follows.

The case of Germany's Chancellor Angela Merkel is particularly instructive. The daughter of a pastor in the former East Germany, Merkel showed no early interest in politics. Instead, she seemed destined for an academic career, her doctorate being in the arcane field of quantum chemistry. The collapse of the Berlin Wall changed all that – and so, critically, did the patronage of Helmut Kohl, the then-Chancellor, who promoted the unknown Merkel and helped her to raise her national profile. Ten years later, however, Merkel authored a blistering attack on her former mentor in the national press, and effectively skewered the man who was responsible for her rise.

Such moments define careers. The skill lies in picking the right moment to strike, and ensuring, in the aftermath, that one's reputation is not irrevocably tarnished or that one's opponents are left damaged but not destroyed.

DON'T RESPOND TO EVERY PROVOCATION

Every single day, we are likely to experience irritating or annoying events when other people seem to be getting their own way or are not giving sufficient attention to our own concerns or priorities. How do we respond to these provocations? Some people will pick a fight at every opportunity, becoming aggressive at each perceived slight or risk of defeat. Such people are quickly labelled troublemakers, forever making a mountain out of a molehill, and they are usually sidelined from positions of influence. Volatility is mostly seen as a liability.

Others don't respond to every defeat with aggression. They 'suck it up', move on with grace and accept that it can be a smart move for others to 'win' some of the time.

The nature of your response to adversity depends on the implications of winning or losing. Just as in tennis, where break points are bigger than merely going 0–15 down, so too in life. If the consequence of defeat is that someone else's ego is assuaged or you are subjected to some minor inconvenience, this is a level-1 infraction – irritating, but not worth putting your reputation on the line for. In other circumstances, however, much more is at stake: a major career opportunity could be missed or one's fundamental values infringed. This is level 3: the klaxon is sounding and your forces should be marshalled for action.

GAUGE YOUR SUPPORT – THEN ACT

If you decide that this is major and you need to act, two competing impulses will often be at play. One is the need for urgency – the window for prevailing against an opponent may be a short one – and the other is the need for deliberation and planning.

It is essential to gauge the strength of support you have for your proposed action. There's no point in waging a war only to find that, in victory, your troops desert you. In the UK, for example, Michael Heseltine famously unseated Prime Minister Margaret Thatcher, but didn't win the subsequent leadership election for himself.

It's also as well to visualize what victory would look like. Are you looking for your view to dominate completely, or is an accommodation with the other side a possibility?

Once these considerations have been addressed, it is time to act. Undue hesitation at such moments will likely consign you to the very long list of might-have-beens. You may feel like waiting until there is a better alignment of interests, that the timing isn't quite right.

It never will be. Catch the wave or miss the moment. It's your choice.

MANAGE THE AFTERMATH

Assuming you win your battle, you will need to ensure stability in the aftermath. Particularly delicate decisions will involve what to do with the vanquished; do you reach an accommodation with whoever you beat, or send them into the wilderness?

Again, the world of politics is instructive here. The biggest, most destructive schism in post-war British politics was not between opposing parties but between the two architects of 'New Labour', Tony Blair and Gordon Brown. Blair of course won the leadership crown that Brown had thought was his by right, but Blair's victory was hollow. The defeated man became a destabilizing influence when the party achieved power, forever undermining and blocking Blair's more radical agenda. Blair had fought and won the leadership battle, but his accommodating stance towards his rival later limited his effectiveness in power. And, in Australia, the festering resentment between party colleagues Kevin Rudd and Julia Gillard turned into farce as first Gillard unseated Rudd, and then Rudd unseated Gillard to become PM a second time.

Winning is not all, then. You need to pay attention to what will happen after you've won, and top of your list of priorities will be how to handle the guy who came second.

Putting it all together

Influence is often won at a cost and, particularly in large organizations, is a zero-sum game. Power is concentrated in the hands of the few and, in order to win your place at the table, you may have to unseat a rival. This is not to suggest that you should actively scheme to ensure a rival's demise, but nor should you assume that rising above the fray is the best way to achieve your objectives. You know what they say about nice guys…

- How easily do you allow minor irritations to unsettle you?
- How aware are you of your level of support?
- Who are your main rivals? Is there room for both of you going forward?

42 Make other people look good

'Give way to your opponent; thus will you gain the crown of victory.' Ovid

'If you are planning on doing business with someone again, don't be too tough in the negotiations. If you are going to skin a cat, don't keep it as a house cat.' Marvin Levin, property developer

'In the best, the friendliest and simplest relations, praise is necessary just as grease is necessary to keep the wheels turning.' Leo Tolstoy, War and Peace

'Appreciation is a wonderful thing. It makes what is excellent in others belong to us as well.' Voltaire

The idea of 'face' is often taken to be an exclusively Asian concept. It's certainly true that anyone who spends any time in, say, China will need to become quickly sensitized to *mianzi*, that set of rituals designed to protect and uphold one's public reputation. The complexity of 'face' often baffles visitors to the region. Even at an intergovernmental level, there is a multitude of ways to get it wrong. During President Hu's 2006 visit to the United States, for example, offence was caused – even if none was intended – by the hosts' provision of a 19-gun salute as opposed to a 21-gun salute; a state luncheon as opposed to a state dinner; and by President Bush tugging at President Hu's jacket as the latter made to leave an official function by the wrong exit. Chinese popular opinion viewed these incidents as slights, marks of disrespect, and the Chinese press gave the trip scant coverage as a result. In appearing to humiliate their leader, the United States had unwittingly humiliated a whole nation.

Face has a far wider application than in the field of cultural studies, however. Acquiring influence – or the right to influence – is a long-term game, and one of its central strategies is earning the trust and respect of those you may one day seek to influence. The best way of doing this is to go out of your way to demonstrate your trust in and respect for them – by helping them avoid loss of face, and taking every opportunity to enhance their reputations.

Making other people look good – or ensuring that they don't lose face – may not always be a top priority in cultures where there is a win-at-all-costs, him-or-me mentality. Here, attention to 'face' may be interpreted as deceitful or contrived – even weakness. Yet showing a concern for the reputation of another is a sure way of earning their gratitude, and making them more disposed to do you a favour in return when you really need it.

HELP PEOPLE LOOK GOOD TO THEIR SUPERIORS

People are under pressure to perform all the time. If you can ease that pressure, or assist with that performance, you will often win a supporter for life. Manisha, a young management consultant, recognized an opportunity to put this into practice with one of her first clients.

'[The client] was on the finance team for a fairly large company and was really worried about giving a presentation to his board. It wasn't a particularly long or complex presentation, but I could tell that the prospect of it was freaking him out. So I took a bit of trouble over helping him with it, drafted it with him, went through the sorts of questions he might be asked. I also talked him through a couple of pieces of research we had done internally which he could present as his own. He aced it on the day, and really grew in confidence because of the positive feedback he got. And he's always remembered that, and introduced me to people and I think pushed internally for us to be used more. So it gave me satisfaction at the time, helping someone out like that, but longer term it has paid off as well.'

It is always worth considering the people your colleagues or clients are trying to impress, and how you can help them do so. The return on investment of time and effort is usually impressive, as the powerful law of reciprocity comes into play, which seems to apply across all cultures and classes. People will remember the favour but will also feel indebted to you; therefore they will be keen to help you out and in so doing clear the 'debt' whenever you choose to call it in.

COMPLIMENT PEOPLE IN PUBLIC

We often feel a sense of foreboding when we hear that we are going to get some 'performance feedback'. Instinctively, we brace ourselves for criticism and start to rehearse in our heads the case for our own defence. The world seems a hostile place at times like these.

That's why positive, public endorsement is so powerful. It has scarcity value. When you publicly support someone by praising their contribution, you are putting your own judgement on the line. It's a big deal. There is, of course, a place for private acknowledgement, the hand on the shoulder and the whispered 'jolly well done'. But in terms of investing in relationships, building other people's confidence and binding them irrevocably to you, nothing beats praise in public – particularly when the subject of your praise is feeling low on confidence.

Machiavellian operators, especially in the field of politics, often use this tactic in reverse: they withhold vocal support. How often have we seen public figures, enduring some torrid spell of bad luck, search in vain for endorsement from their colleagues? In these scenarios, rivals regard silence as the more potent tool for their own advancement. One also needs to be aware of the demotivating effect public praise can have on the colleagues of the person praised.

But praise a person in public and you can rely on their support in future. It is a technique that sometimes requires a conscious change in the way we view the world, however – many of us find it easier to find fault with others than appreciate their virtues.

ALLOW OTHERS A WAY OUT WITH DIGNITY

Sometimes we find ourselves dealt a particularly strong hand in an interaction. We hold most of the aces. The temptation in such a situation is to exploit our position for all it is worth, to grind our opponent into the dust. This is rarely a good idea, as history has too often shown. Seeking to impose a draconian settlement on the losing side encourages resentment and thirst for revenge to fester. Your victory may be short-lived, as the peacemakers at Versailles could testify.

It is better by far to consider ways to help your opponent retreat with dignity – to save face in the truest sense. The thought of outright defeat can often lead to stalemate, as those who believe they have nothing left to lose prevaricate and disrupt. Think about a solution that means they can reasonably claim to have won something from the discussion, and you will often achieve your objectives more quickly, leaving no toxic legacy of distrust.

Human interactions are rarely a zero-sum game, where I can only win if you comprehensively lose.

Putting it all together

It may seem counterintuitive to conclude that one of the best ways to succeed is by helping others taste success. But what goes around comes around. The more time and effort we devote to making other people look good, the greater the pool of goodwill we create for ourselves when we need it most. It is a long-term investment strategy, one that requires us to surrender our self-absorption and delve deeply into the motivations and insecurities of others.

The effective influencer is always looking two or three steps ahead – thinking about what the consequences would be if this friend became a foe or in what circumstances this person's assistance might yet prove decisive – and never more so than in the effective application of this tactic. That is not to say that making other people look good is entirely a cynical, self-interested ploy; rather, the successful influencer will seek out opportunities to do others a good turn. It demonstrates compassion, which in itself is laudable; and it also offers long-term leverage, which no influencer would eschew.

- Instead of asking what's in for you, ask first what's in it for them.
- Make a point of actively seeking the positive in other people's everyday performance.
- Help someone avoid embarrassment or humiliation and you will win their gratitude for ever.

43 Control the process

'Tomorrow's battle is won during today's practice.' Japanese proverb

'The will to win is important, but the will to prepare is vital.' Joe Paterno

'Chaos is merely order waiting to be deciphered.' José Saramago

'He listens well who takes notes.' Dante Alighieri

'The sublimity of administration consists in knowing the proper degree of power that should be exerted on different occasions.' Charles de Montesquieu

Sheer, dazzling brilliance and astonishing inventiveness are clearly useful if you want to be influential. Fortunately for the lesser mortals among us, they are not the only routes to influence.

Whenever decisions need to be made or agreements reached, there is always a process to be managed. Participants need to be corralled. Information needs to be assimilated. Discussions need to be recorded. Decisions need to be prioritized and implemented. And this process – the painstaking business of converting talk into action – presents a real opportunity for anyone with the administrative skill to facilitate it.

Administration is often considered a dirty word and yet some of the greatest influencers of all time have been administrators: Machiavelli himself and Thomas Cromwell, to name but two. They were not in the limelight but were highly effective aides to the principals. They saw their role as staying in the shadows, implementing their master's orders as efficiently as possible and quietly building their knowledge of how things really get done.

Despite these precedents, we don't need to think of administration as entirely sinister; indeed, it performs a valuable service in ensuring that decisions get made and work gets done. And the need for the service shouldn't be underestimated. Whenever people gather in discourse, there is potential for misunderstanding, convolution and digression. Keeping people on track is an art in short supply. Likewise, holding people accountable for their actions, ensuring that there is some follow-up when decisions have apparently been made, can confer as much visibility and significance on the diligent administrator as on the principals themselves.

Even if you don't have a clear role, voting rights or line authority, you can still affect an outcome by taking responsibility for the 'nitty-gritty' – the stuff no one wants to put their hand up for but without which agreement would never be reached, decisions would not be implemented and progress would never be made.

TAKE THE NOTES

Taking the notes in meetings is often the role doled out to the most junior person present, which is interesting because it seems to imply a low-status function. In the British Cabinet, by contrast, the person who takes the notes is the Cabinet Secretary, the highest-ranking official in the British civil service. Maybe it is a role that should be sought after rather than avoided.

Who said what and when are vital observations in any decision-making process. The opportunity that note-taking responsibility gives is not in any sense to massage or manipulate the record, but to act as go-between after the fact. Things need checking, actions need allocating and follow-up appointments need to be diarized. All these give plentiful opportunity to converse quite legitimately with the major actors at a meeting or on a call. If you become known as an effective note-taker – meticulous, well organized – you will probably find key decision makers come to rely on you. Everyone wants their point of view accurately reported: if you can do it, people will value you.

Another great advantage of being the note-taker is that it gives you access to important conversations without necessarily having any obligation to contribute. You are the witness to events, not their architect. This means that you get to see how people operate and gain an insight into how they prefer to argue or be influenced, which can be useful intelligence for the future.

BE THE TIMEKEEPER

Time is everyone's most valuable commodity, but you'd never guess it from the way most meetings are managed. Many of us spend hours of most working days sitting in meetings thinking: 'Why am I here?' The agenda seems vague or non-existent; certain individuals monopolize discussion or tell us things they've told us a dozen times before; participants are late; or the meeting runs over. Hell is truly someone else's meeting.

But who says any of this? Who takes a meeting by the scruff of the neck, quietening the chatterboxes and keeping the thing on track? Here is an opportunity for you to exert some influence.

'I remember getting really frustrated with the way meetings were run in our organization,' says Alice, a marketing manager, 'and so I resolved to do something about it. I would say to people who were going off the point, "Sorry, but that's not what we're here to discuss." I wouldn't tolerate any of this waiting around for people who were habitually late... I would speak to them beforehand and say, look, we're scheduled to meet for half an hour, and that's all we're getting." I thought I would appal people but I've got some of the best feedback ever as a result of it. Literally, people would come up afterwards and say, "Thank God you shut so-and-so up, he's been driving me crazy for years..."'

SUMMARIZE

Forcing people to focus is critical if interactions, be they meetings or phone calls, are not to become mere talking shops. Because the temptation to ramble, to stray well away from the point, is irresistible for some participants, you need to find a way to bring a meeting to order. The well-judged summary is an excellent device for doing this graciously: it demonstrates that you have been listening, allows the possibility of clarification, and permits you to stamp your authority on an interaction even if you have not been doing most of the talking.

Good non-confrontational ways of performing the vital public service of keeping a discussion on track including saying the following:

- 'Can we just take stock...?'
- 'What we seem to be saying is...'
- 'Maybe it would helpful if I recap where we seem to have got to so far...'

These can be particularly useful when a discussion gets heated or when one or two participants are dominating.

One of our interviewees remembered his mentor fondly:

'The great thing about Robert's style of influence was that it was so understated. He wouldn't be the loudest voice in meetings, or do most of the talking. But he would be there guiding the outcomes in a very subtle way. He was great at gently interrupting people who had been talking too much by saying "John, let me just make sure I've got the gist of what you're saying ... because I'm sure that Alison has got something important to add to it..." He was a great facilitator, not dominating a meeting with ego but making sure everyone's views were heard.'

To be a great facilitator of interaction between people demands that you suppress your own ego – it's very difficult to notice the ebbs and flows of conversations if you tend to monopolize them – and that you adopt the position of guardian of the outcome. Your influence is used to ensure that an outcome is achieved and actioned, however the participants may try to impede this.

Your toolkit will involve the less talked-about techniques of refocusing, summarizing and cajoling. It is not glamorous work, but if your efforts save people time and achieve results, you can acquire as much influence as the greatest and loudest grandstander.

- When did you last offer to take the notes in a meeting? What are the possibilities for following up with the principals to clarify the points they were making?
- How can you keep people on track in a polite way?
- Do you read the body language in meetings? If you notice that people are getting bored, can you use a summary to bring focus to the discussion?

44 Pull the plug – quickly

> 'The hardest thing is to let go of a player who has been a great guy – but all the evidence is on the field. If you see the change, the deterioration, you have to ask yourself what things are going to be like two years ahead.' Sir Alex Ferguson

> 'Bad news isn't wine. It doesn't improve with age.' Colin Powell, former US Secretary of State

> 'Kill your darlings, kill your darlings, even when it breaks your egocentric little scribbler's heart, kill your darlings.' Stephen King, On Writing

> 'Mr Corleone is a man who insists on hearing bad news immediately.' Tom Hagen to Woltz, The Godfather

> 'He behaved like an ostrich and put his head in the sand, thereby exposing his thinking parts.' George Carman, barrister, on the behaviour of a defendant

You have invested heavily in the launch of a new product. It has taken a couple of years to get it off the ground, what with all the market research and product testing. And now, six months after launch, the sales figures aren't looking good. Your marketing team is in favour of changing the ad agency and the product guys say there is a need for additional functionality. You look at the spend so far: nearly a million. That's a huge amount to write off. It would be better, surely, to authorize the additional expenditure, cross your fingers and hope things turn around quickly?

You are a sports-team coach. Your team is experiencing a slump in form and confidence. Results have not been good. At training, you notice that one of the players – the captain, no less – seems to have lost a bit of pace, a bit of presence. It's nothing drastic, but you can see he's not quite on his game. Still, what's one poor season in an otherwise glittering career? He'll bounce back. The old magic can't have disappeared. He's still the first name you put on the team sheet…

As children, we grow accustomed to happy endings. Books and films convince us that, whatever obstacles we face, things turn out all right in the end. Some of that expectation transfers to adulthood. If we find ourselves in a hole, we often persuade ourselves that a few more hours' digging will lead us to the trapdoor that takes us to the tunnel that will magic us to the desert island, the lobster salad, the pina colada…

Confirmation bias is a well-established psychological phenomenon: we see what we want to see and disregard the rest. To pay full attention to bad news, to confront uncomfortable truths and their consequences, is to court unpopularity, to spoil the party.

Sometimes, though, you need to burst that bubble. Hiding your head in the sand can ultimately make a bad situation a whole lot worse. So how acute is your sense for the tipping point, the moment when to defer or delay an unpopular decision is likely to create an even bigger disaster? At such moments, do you tend to stick or twist?

Pulling the plug on people, projects and pipe dreams will not win you popularity, but over time it is likely to garner you respect. It takes courage, foresight and pragmatism – all attributes of the truly influential.

LOOK FOR PATTERNS IN EARLY-STAGE EVIDENCE

A hunch is not a fact, but it is remarkable how many decisions are made on the basis of hunches, and how many decisions fail to be made despite overwhelming factual evidence. The pharmaceutical industry, for example, is well known for authorizing ever more expensive clinical trials for products known from the outset to be flawed. (See AstraZeneca's experience with the drug Fostamatinib as a case in point.) The lure of discovering the new blockbuster drug seems to blind decision makers to the facts.

Likewise, you can probably remember a car journey to somewhere in the middle of nowhere, which ended up being the road trip from hell. Every twist and turn of the road told you that you were not getting any nearer your destination. Did you stop and retrace your tracks or carry on regardless, hope triumphing over experience?

A single bit of bad news or disappointing evidence may mean little, but a pattern or a trend is a different thing altogether. Look out for such patterns; use them to start to question basic assumptions about projects. This may be unpopular; you may risk accusations of damaging morale. But influential people know the cost of minor mistakes turning into damaging disasters, and will gladly suffer short-term unpopularity to avoid long-term reputational damage.

FIRE PEOPLE

If it seems difficult to stop a project in its tracks, it often feels impossible to do the same with people. We will offer chronic underperformers second or third chances, remedial coaching, time off in lieu – anything rather than face the inescapable conclusion that someone's performance has dipped below an acceptable level and that it is unlikely to recover any time soon.

I am not advocating a 'one strike and you're out' attitude. Of course, you will give underperforming colleagues a chance to address their issues. But when do a few instances of underperformance become a trend? And at what point does the trend become irreversible? Assuming you can identify this point, is your instinct to deny, defer or act?

Firing people is important if you are to acquire true influence because it demonstrates courage – unless you delegate the task to the HR department, whereupon it demonstrates weakness – and it also sets a precedent.

'The best thing I ever did was fire a chronic underperformer,' reflects Tom, a senior manager in a manufacturing company. 'Number one, it distinguished me from my predecessors who had just let the situation slide because they didn't want the confrontation. And two, it put down a marker for the sort of standards I expect. Many managers espouse high standards but don't enforce them. You have to be willing to get rid of the dead wood.'

WELCOME – AND INSIST ON RECEIVING – BAD NEWS

All this assumes that you have plenty of evidence at your disposal as projects evolve or teams grow, but frequently this not the case. Either your own confirmation bias is at work, ensuring that you ignore or avoid evidence that conflicts with your desired outcome, or people around you just don't feel able to bring you bad news. The latter is a symptom of a closed or defensive culture, where past experience proves that any messenger bearing bad news tends to get shot. It is also inevitable that the higher you rise in an organization, the more distant you get from these golden nuggets of real-time feedback.

It is important to show that, although you don't shirk from firing people for underperformance, bringing you bad news is certainly not a sackable offence. Welcome it, seek it out and weigh the good stuff against the bad. This applies whether you are gauging team morale or managing discrete projects. Ensure that you are not insulated from bad news – by wandering around, using lots of different people as sounding boards and even encouraging anonymous feedback or suggestions.

Putting it all together

Inertia is often justified by reference to the oil tanker metaphor: this thing is just so big that to stop it, far less turn it around, is impractical; better leave well alone until it reaches its destination.

The truth is that oil tankers **can** be stopped and turned around, and so can your project, your team or your career. The world of hi tech start-ups has introduced to common parlance the concept of the 'pivot' – that crucial phase of any embryonic business when it responds to early-stage feedback and changes course or shuts down as necessary. Without an early-stage pivot, Starbucks would still be selling coffee beans to retailers and YouTube would still be an online dating site. These early business models didn't work, so the founders pulled the plug and tried something new. Being receptive to this kind of feedback, and being flexible enough to act on it even if there is a cost in human terms, is a powerful and unusual mindset.

Sometimes, in life and in business, you just have to be cruel to be kind.

- Do you pay enough attention to early-stage feedback?
- Do you weigh the good news and the bad news dispassionately?
- When did you last take the decision to 'kill' a project – and how did you defend your decision to the disappointed, the disillusioned and the disenfranchised?

45 Promote yourself

> 'Sell yourself first if you want to sell anything.' Burt Lancaster

> 'If you really put a small value upon yourself, rest assured that the world will not raise your price.' Unknown

> 'Believe in yourself! Have faith in your abilities! Without a humble but reasonable confidence in your own powers you cannot be successful or happy.' Norman Vincent Peale

> 'If you ask men why they did a good job, they'll say, "I'm awesome. Obviously. Why are you even asking?" If you ask women why they did a good job, what they'll say is someone helped them, they got lucky, they worked really hard.' Sheryl Sandberg

> 'Life is one big pitch, so you better start practising.' Dan Schawbel

Alison, a mid-level manager at a recruitment agency, was fed up with the message she kept receiving at appraisal time.

'It was always the same. They told me I was doing very well, was highly regarded, but needed to get out and "sell myself" more. It used to frustrate the hell out of me, because firstly I thought the work should stand up for itself and secondly the thought of "selling myself" turned me into a gibbering wreck…'

There is little point in doing high-quality work if no one knows that it was yours. You need to take responsibility for how the rest of the organization sees you, and that will involve some proactive self-promotion. This is the page where less demonstrative types will file this book in the nearest wastepaper basket in horror. But 'self-promotion' here doesn't mean self-aggrandizing speeches or indiscriminate sucking up or schmoozing. It simply means ensuring that you receive the credit that's due to you – and for that to happen, people need to know who you are and what you have done.

Key here is that you are promoting yourself via your achievements, not your dazzling personality or good looks. Influence attaches itself to people with a demonstrable track record of walking the talk, but that certainly doesn't mean that the work 'speaks for itself'.

There is evidence to suggest that men are, on the whole, more comfortable with this than women. If you find the prospect of talking about yourself simply intolerable, you may need to find someone who will do your promotion for you, as Alison eventually discovered:

'I was really lucky to find a mentor who would "mention me in dispatches", as he put it – let people know that I had done a good job in emails, invite me to give updates on what I was doing at departmental meetings, especially when he knew we had just won a big account, that kind of thing. And eventually I got a bit more used to finding opportunities to discuss what I've been up to. I usually do it by updating colleagues on things I've discovered during client conversations that may be of use to them. At the same time, of course, they get to hear about the work I've done, but it's a subtler approach that works for me.'

REFINE YOUR ELEVATOR PITCH

Every time you introduce yourself is an opportunity to sell yourself. Instead, people often manage to combine squirming embarrassment with impenetrable mumble when announcing themselves to a new group or contact. In the old days of the dotcom boom, everyone was supposed to have an 'elevator pitch': a pithy line that summarized their attributes in the time it took the elevator to reach the C-suite. We might not be pitching to VCs in our day-to-day work, but it still makes sense to work out a more compelling introduction than 'I'm, er, Kathy from upstairs.'

Highlight the people you help as well as your job title – and briefly outline a recent project or achievement. So Kathy might add: 'I'm the marketing manager for the region, so one of the things I do is help our fee earners put together pitches and find ways of winning new business. Last week, for example, we managed to secure a new account with…'

The advantage of this approach is twofold:

- It positions you as the go-to person for pitches and winning new business.
- It provides an opportunity for the other person to find out more about your latest success and to walk away with a sense of you as an achiever.

JOIN THINGS AND OFFER YOUR HELP FIRST

Your normal daily interactions may provide you with enough opportunities to discuss your current work and give people a sense of your recent achievements. But if you work for yourself or within a very small team, the possibilities for self-promotion are far more limited. In this situation, you will need to manufacture opportunities to discuss what you do by joining up with other people.

Volunteers are always being sought for this, that or the other. These requests come in the sorts of emails we tend to delete without thinking – we don't have time to do the things we are paid to do, let alone take on new commitments. But profile raising is like a pyramid scheme: we need an initial set of interactions to touch off many more. The smaller your natural milieu, the more you will need to seek out new fora in which to introduce yourself.

Charity work, sports teams, professional associations and alumni groupings all provide great opportunities to spread the word. You can describe what you do, outline recent achievements and make it clear what future opportunities you are on the lookout for. You get the chance to do this by employing the rule of reciprocity: go first, ask about other people and how you can help them, and by and large they will return the favour.

PROMOTE YOURSELF BY PROXY

When you just can't conquer your natural modesty, or there don't seem to be any suitable opportunities for you to gently toot your own horn, you may need to enlist some help. Ask a friend, colleague, supporter or sponsor to draw attention to your achievements. Alison, whom we met at the start of the chapter, had success with just this approach.

'I was really lucky in that I had a mentor who would send emails thanking me for contributions to certain things and would copy in a couple of other senior managers; or, when we received some decent client feedback, he would forward that on to other people. So it was quite subtle, not in your face, but a method of promoting me and making people aware of my capabilities in a way I couldn't do myself, or wouldn't feel comfortable doing myself.'

Putting it all together

Asking other people to 'put a good word in' is one of the specific influence-building tactics that a recent McKinsey survey found came much more naturally to men than to women. But calling in a favour, leveraging your network, being quite blunt about how your contacts can help you – this is the approach you may need to consider if the world is going to hear about how good you are and you don't want to do it yourself.

- How do you introduce yourself and what you do to strangers?
- What forums have you joined with the express intention of getting better known?
- Can someone influential help raise your profile?

46 Negotiate

'All over the world when you test men and women for facial
cue recognition, women test [...] better. It's a negotiation tool.'
Michael Gurian

'Don't bargain yourself down before you get to the table.'
Carol Frohlinger

'You must never try to make all the money that's in a deal. Let
the other fellow make some money too, because if you have
a reputation for always making all the money, you won't have
many deals.' **J. Paul Getty**

'When the final result is expected to be a compromise, it is often
prudent to start from an extreme position.' **John Maynard Keynes**

'He who has learned to disagree without being disagreeable
has discovered the most valuable secret of a diplomat.'
Robert Estabrook

Outside observers will sometimes attribute an individual's level
of influence to a random mix of charisma, opportunism and luck.
The person was born that way, they are suggesting, or the lucky
breaks just happened to fall into their laps. What we could be
severely underestimating in these circumstances is the extent to
which influence was acquired, over time, through negotiation.

It is dangerous to generalize too much, but it is fair to say that
most of the people I interviewed for this book had a couple of
beliefs in common. The first was that *they believed their lot could*

always be improved – be that through salary, status or whatever metric they used. The second belief was that the improvement would only come *directly from their own actions* – if they wanted a bigger slice of the pie, they would have to ask for it. It wasn't going to be handed to them on some sort of meritocratic plate. Several people were at pains to point out that there comes a point where, if you are not happy with your lot, you need to 'stick your neck out'.

There is a certain amount of academic research to suggest that this approach generally comes more easily to men than women. A famous study that monitored attitudes to asking for a pay rise found that while 85 per cent of men were happy to measure their worth in monetary terms, 83 per cent of women were uncomfortable doing so. Women believed that if they did a good job the organization would reward them. Men believed they had to advocate for themselves.[1] When Carnegie-Mellon professor Linda Babcock asked men and women to choose from a list of metaphors to describe how they felt about the prospect of negotiating, the men's top pick was 'winning a ball game'. The women's was 'going to the dentist'.

It may be that, if you are not getting the influence you want, you are simply not asking for it.

Influence is not necessarily won by chance or stealth; it is seized. And becoming a confident negotiator, particularly on your own behalf, may be one of the most crucial skill sets of all.

DON'T SETTLE

When was the last time the deal you were offered wasn't the one you wanted? Maybe it was a salary discussion. Maybe it was being shown to a table in a restaurant.

What did you do? Negotiate – or settle?

There are a plethora of social and cultural norms that prevent us negotiating in circumstances like this, not to mention our own

---

1 'Ask and you shall receive? Gender differences in negotiators' beliefs', *Human Relations* 56.6: 625

self-limiting beliefs. 'It would be rude to argue.' 'I will come across as brash/arrogant/bossy if I try to ask for more.'

Influential people find a way of overcoming these limitations. Based usually on a sound sense of their own worth, these people regard the offers that are made to them, the deals that are presented, as a starting point. If they don't like the starting point, they negotiate.

The restaurant situation proved revelatory for Katherine, a healthcare professional:

'I always seemed to get shown to the worst table in restaurants – the one next to the loo or next to the kitchen. And I would just dutifully sit where I was told and spend the whole meal moaning about it. One day I just said, "Would you mind if we sat somewhere else – like there for example?" And the waiter just shrugged and said, "Sure." Sounds stupid, but it was a light-bulb moment. It's true: if you don't ask, you don't get.'

We tend to think of negotiation as a formal process, taking place in the boardroom in the presence of legal advisers. In fact, it's an everyday occurrence; whenever we feel there are more options to consider and a better outcome to be had, a negotiation can take place. The first step is to realize this and to start the conversation.

MAKE THE OPENING OFFER

Even on the occasions when we are prepared to negotiate, we sometimes scupper the outcome by ceding the initiative at an early stage. Perhaps we have the paradigm of the canny poker player in our minds: we play our cards very close to our chest, giving away nothing and responding instead to the opening moves of our opponent.

An increasing body of evidence suggests that this is not the way to secure the best deal. Going first takes advantage of the powerful effect of 'anchoring', which Daniel Kahneman and others have explored: you set the terms of the discussion and the other side will be obliged to play within your boundaries. This approach makes you seem confident and well prepared, and you are also strategically placed to make the first concession. You can be flexible; you have built-in room to manoeuvre. By contrast, if you find yourself on the back foot, responding to someone else's low offer, you have only the limited choices of making a very small concession or walking away.

A couple of traps to avoid when making the first offer are:

- aiming low
- offering a range of alternatives.

Deference plays its part here: we don't want to appear too 'pushy', so we deliberately aim for the mid-range of our best expectations. And just in case we appear too opportunistic, we may even preface our offer with something like, 'To start us off, I think I'm looking for budget increase of between 2 and 4 per cent.' This will, of course, focus attention at the lower end of the range; it would have been better to start the discussion at 4 per cent.

In negotiations, always aim high and shoot first.

KEEP PLENTY OF PLATES SPINNING

Zero-sum negotiations leave a nasty taste in the mouth. When we fix on a single outcome – a figure, say, in salary negotiations – and when we are convinced that there is only one possible result that we will be happy with, we engage in a confrontational negotiation where one party wins and the other loses. Clearly, this isn't helpful if we have to maintain relations with the other party regardless of the outcome.

It is better to keep an open mind and look to broaden the scope of the discussion. Perhaps if we work towards a 'package' outcome rather than defeat or victory on a single issue, we will achieve a win–win and actually strengthen a relationship rather than poison it permanently.

It may be that in a budget negotiation, for example, there are alternatives to getting fixated on a headline figure. Perhaps the timescale can be looked at, with any reductions being phased; perhaps longer-term return on investment can be assessed; maybe there are parts of the business that are likely to turn a profit, and both cost and profit centres can be addressed simultaneously.

In the classic terminology this is called 'expanding the pie' rather than merely slicing it. In a salary negotiation, this means that money would be discussed along with hours, benefits and work–life balance. Perhaps what you lose on the roundabouts you gain on the swings.

Putting it all together

Being seen to be a successful and willing negotiator has two impacts on influence. The first is direct – you are more likely to win for yourself a bigger share of the pie than would be possible by just keeping your fingers crossed. The second is less direct but more important. Effective negotiators are perceived as powerful, confident and influential. The mere fact that you are not willing always to accept what you are given is impressive in the eyes of others, particularly if, as well as negotiating for your own benefit, you have a track record of doing so for others.

- When did you last refuse to accept what you were given?
- What would an opening offer sound like if you were to aim high in your next negotiation?
- How successful are you at expanding as well as slicing the cake?

47 Always be campaigning

> 'Anyone who says they are not interested in politics is like a drowning man who insists he is not interested in water.' Mahatma Gandhi

> 'I'm not the smartest fellow in the world, but I can sure pick smart colleagues.' Franklin D. Roosevelt

> 'Whoever said, "It's not whether you win or lose that counts" probably lost.' Martina Navratilova

The legendary speech by Alec Baldwin in **Glengarry Glen Ross** got it wrong. It's not the Closing that matters; it's the Campaigning.

Whenever I bring up the word 'politics' in a workshop and relate it to the workplace, the vast majority of people tend (metaphorically!) to hold their nose and look away. There is a huge distaste for the concept, with its obvious Machiavellian overtones. At the same time, everyone is aware that it is a fact of life and that, ultimately, in any environment involving more than two people, you have a stark choice: play, or be played.

Let's be clear. If you have any leadership ambitions at all, you will need to build a following. This does not take place overnight, as any political pundit will tell you. The time to start winning the next election is immediately after you fought the last.

You have limited time for this activity, particularly in an early stage of your career, when any overt impression of electioneering will be regarded with disdain in any case. Any activity you do undertake will need to be focused and discreet – but it will need to take place. Positions of influence, like elections, are never won overnight.

In terms of using your time efficiently, you can learn a lot from the way political campaigns are orchestrated. The electorate is segmented into supporters, opponents and the up-for-grabs. You will use different tactics for each category, but suffice to say you will spend most your time wooing the undecided, who could hold the key to your ascent.

Politics, while in my view inevitable, don't have to be dirty. They are simply a means to an end: in this case the end is providing you with enough power and influence to achieve whatever it is you want to achieve. It isn't necessarily manipulative or malign. It is the process by which things get done whenever quantities of people are involved. If the thought of being a politician appals, you may need to wave goodbye to any aspirations of influence.

FIND A CHIEF OF STAFF

Beyond the select circle of people who harbour genuine leadership ambitions lies another subset: those who have limited ambitions themselves but who see themselves in the 'kingmaker' role. They want to access to power, but without necessarily accepting the responsibility of it. If you add to the mix a good work ethic and outstanding organizational ability, you have an asset worth its weight in gold. In all my research into people who have reached a position of leadership within an organization, very few have not had a 'trusted lieutenant', whether assigned an official title or working quietly away from the limelight. They are your eyes and ears, your sounding board, your cheerleader in chief.

It is understandable, but not entirely smart, to choose someone as your chief of staff simply because you feel comfortable with them. Personality fit is not necessarily the only criterion for this critical role. They need perspective and a high level of political acumen: you may need to buy in such expertise.

A managing partner of an international law firm told us:

'I did need someone to help me reach this position and, once here, execute what I needed to. I actually hired a guy from our closest competitor for that very purpose. I knew taking on this other firm would be a successful strategy for me personally and for our firm, and clearly having someone with that level of inside knowledge was very helpful.'

Final thought: you need to be pretty sure about the chief of staff's own leadership ambitions or rather lack of them. You don't want your number two destabilizing your leadership. It happens. Ask former UK Prime Minister Tony Blair.

IDENTIFY YOUR OPPONENTS

If you don't have any opponents, you must be doing something wrong. Anyone who takes a view, advocates change or looks somehow to disrupt the status quo will encounter opposition from the entrenched advocates of inertia. If you have not upset anyone, you are clearly not making an impact.

It is unlikely that implacable opponents can be 'won round', so it is wasted energy trying to do so. It is very worth while trying to understand their position, though, either through polite conversation initiated by you, or by what is reported back to you by your supporters. Understanding an opponent's perspective is more important than making the chemistry work. You are probably never going to be best buddies, but achieving your aims in the longer term may require an accommodation with him.

Here is the managing partner again:

'Rising through the ranks, you definitely get a sense of who your rivals are. I have always tried to avoid it becoming personal – I have had about three rows since I got here 20 years ago. So it is brisk, it is businesslike. I don't waste a lot of time on it – but I make sure I know what they are up to and now that I am in the leadership position, I will make a point of consulting them and asking them to chair meetings. It's important for the culture of the place that I am seen to be inclusive. I don't harbour grudges.'

DEVOTE TIME TO THE NON-ALIGNEDS

In politics, it's all about the floating voters. People with leadership aspirations often fail to devote enough time to canvassing the views of the non-aligned, but if you can get enough of them around to your way of thinking, the keys to the kingdom can be yours.

Floating voters are notoriously fickle. You think they're in your pocket one day, only to find that they have transferred their support to another suitor. That's why the title of this chapter is 'Always be campaigning'; to be sure of people's support, you need to be checking in with them on a regular basis.

One person we interviewed made a point every week of reconnecting with five individuals whom he had not seen or talked to recently. Another divisional head made a point of holding regular 'brown bag' lunches where anyone could just pitch up and hear him give an overview of what was going on in the team – and ask him a question.

There is a two-part approach to the winning over of floating voters – which in any event is incremental over time. In the main, it seems to be important to create opportunities to listen to what they have to say. (MPs in the UK hold regular monthly 'surgeries' for their constituents for just this reason.) The second part is to undertake to help them resolve their issues. There is no 'canvassing' of your own views at all.

One interviewee recalled one specific example of this.

'I remember, just after I made director, that I asked to go along to a meeting of the IT team. Now these folks were among the most maligned in the whole organization. And I had to listen to a stream of vitriol about how they were under-appreciated and under-resourced. And there were a few things I undertook to look into, and one of the results was that I managed to get management buy-in for a software upgrade they had been recommending. Well, now I am MD they are just great with me. The service I get from them is outstanding and I think they have fought my corner with other support services. Just showing these people a bit of TLC has had an big pay-off.'

Putting it all together

Do you play or not? You have the option of refusing to 'schmooze' and of not caring what your opponents think. The difficulty with this approach will come when you need to gather support – if, for example, you want a project to get off the ground, you want to position yourself for promotion, or you want a bigger say in how things are run. Then it becomes a numbers game, just as much as any election. And the would-be influential, for all their disdain of politicians, cannot remain entirely aloof from organizational politics.

- Who can you rely on to watch your back? Do you have someone who fulfils the chief-of-staff role?
- Who are your main opponents? How well do you know their world?
- What system do you have in place for listening to the grievances of 'floating voters'?

Start a revolution

> 'It's the action, not the fruit of the action, that's important. You have to do the right thing. It may not be in your power, may not be in your time, that there'll be any fruit. But that doesn't mean you stop doing the right thing. You may never know what results come from your action. But if you do nothing, there will be no result.' **Mahatma Gandhi**

> 'I was tired of being treated like a second-class citizen.' **Rosa Parks**

> 'Perhaps as an old man I will take great comfort in pottering around in a lab and gently talking to students in the summer evening and will accept suffering with insouciance. But not now: men in their prime, if they have convictions, are tasked to act on them.' Julian Assange

> 'Sometimes, the only way to gain your superior's respect is to defy him.' **Kevin Spacey** as **Francis Underwood**, *House of Cards*

> 'And to those who would choose the safety of inaction over the danger of taking a stand, I have this to say: You bloody cowards. May you have the world that you deserve.' **Mira Grant**

Some of the most influential figures in history came to public attention through acts of defiance.

- In Raj-era India, Mahatma Gandhi initiated his Salt March in defiance of the salt taxes imposed by the British. He led his followers to the sea and gathered his own salt, thereby proclaiming, he said, the end of the British Empire.

- In December 1955, Rosa Parks refused to give up her seat to a white man on a bus in Montgomery, Alabama. In doing so, she violated the laws of segregation in force at the time – and became one of the most important symbols of the Civil Rights Movement in America.
- More recently, Julian Assange, whatever you think of the morality of WikiLeaks, showed the level of profile that is possible when you defy authority.

Clearly, these acts of defiance are on a grand scale, but they have lessons for any would-be influencer. Sometimes you have to have the courage of your convictions and you have to make a stand. This doesn't have to be at the macro level of fundamental human rights. It can be decidedly micro: a client of mine earned considerable kudos by insisting on a better standard of catering at his firm's cafeteria. He says that he's better known for the chilli prawn linguini than any of the deals he's brought in over the years.

The point about making a stand is that it demonstrates courage, not a quality in wide circulation. It may earn you unpopularity in certain quarters, but it will also win you respect.

Most people do nothing more than whinge about their lot. Are you prepared to take a risk and be a little more provocative?

DEFY YOUR BOSS

It's true that many senior people like to surround themselves with yes men. If this is the case with your boss, then treat this strategy with caution! However, there are also many leaders who welcome dissent, or who at least have a grudging respect for it on the rare occasions that it happens.

When you are asked to follow a strategy you believe to be misguided, or to endorse a decision you think is plain wrong, you have a choice: stick or twist. Before expressing your misgivings, some calculations are required:

- How important is this to you? Defiance is risky – only do it when it really matters.
- How important is this to your boss? Shooting down a personal pet project may be unwise.

- How much support do you have? It'll be you in the firing line on the ground – but make sure you have some air cover.

Julie, a marketing director, has used the strategy and prospered because of it:

'Without doubt, I owe a lot of my success to my willingness to challenge people. It actually helps being a woman in a very male environment, I think. Firstly, the guys are so nervous of being seen to be excluding a female voice that they hear me out even when I make quite provocative remarks. Secondly, I really do think I see things differently, and they will often say, "I hadn't thought of it like that..." If I didn't challenge, I believe they would implement a less good solution.'

RAISE STANDARDS

Despite the best of intentions, in any team, over time, standards slip and complacency creeps in. The stock response to any questioning of this is usually cynicism: 'What do you expect?' 'C'est la vie.' 'Some things never change.'

It doesn't have to be this way. Nowhere is it written that you have to settle for second class, second rate or second place.

Challenging authority in defence of a personal principle takes courage. Doing so to improve the quality of other people's performance can be even more formidable. Vested interests may squeal, but you have to believe that over time results will repay the upheaval.

A professional sports coach told us about the way he made an impression on his new charges:

'For me, it was all about standards. There was a culture at the club of sloppiness. People arrived for training ten minutes late, and when you questioned them about it would just shrug and say, "No one's ever talked about punctuality before." We had a photocall and people turned up wearing lots of different kit, which I wasn't happy with. I'm a firm believer that you have to attack the "good enough" mentality, the laziness. A lot of what

I've picked up on clearly went unnoticed under the last manager but for me the little stuff influences the big stuff.'

Again, this is influence by differentiation. It's so much easier to go with the flow – to regard the slide to the bottom as inevitable and unstoppable. It's a rare person who raises their hand and says, 'Wait a minute...', but it's the hunch that actually things could be better, and the courage to say so, that marks out the influential from the mediocre.

CALL TIME

Sometimes it's not a principle or a standard that needs you to stand up and be counted. It's time. The propensity to waste time – their own and other people's – is a trap that many people seem only too happy to fall into. Think back on last week. How much time did you spend silently cursing the never-ending meeting, the entirely unnecessary phone call, the email trail you have been unfathomably copied in on?

Why remain silent? Shout stop!

Cold calls are the bane of many people's lives – they are an interruption, a waste of our time and an invasion of privacy. In the UK, it is possible to register your landline so that, in theory, you won't receive any, but the system doesn't always work. A celebrated case in 2012 attracted the attention of the national media when a homeowner who had registered his number was so enraged by the number of cold calls he still kept receiving from insurance companies that he made a note of the time he was wasting answering their calls and put in a claim for compensation. Two aspects of this are particularly noteworthy: the first is that he took action rather than just moaning; the second is that his claim was successful.

As the individual concerned commented, in words which should inspire us all:

'It cheered me up to think that instead of being the victim of these calls I can actually defend myself against them to put the boot on the other foot.'

Putting it all together

If you want to be influential, you need to stop settling for second best. Avoid the trap of 'learned helplessness' and voice the anger that other people are surely feeling but are too afraid to express. Be a spokesperson, a rebel, an agitator. You might want to do this sparingly, and only in situations where you can see clearly that the advantages of winning outweigh the disadvantages of losing. But any study of the truly influential will show that they were more willing than most to stand up and be counted rather than settle for an easy – but unsatisfactory – daily life.

- When did you last disagree with your boss? Are you genuinely valued for the point of view you bring – even if it clashes with the hierarchy?
- What standards do you know for sure have slipped in your professional or personal life? What do you intend to do about it?
- When did you last call out someone for wasting your time?

49 Leave at the top

> 'The secret to a long life's knowing when it's time to go...'
> Michelle Shocked, *Texas Campfire Tapes*

> 'Nothing in his life became him like the leaving of it.'
> William Shakespeare, Macbeth

> 'Quit while you're ahead. All the best gamblers do.' Baltasar Gracian

> 'Affairs are easier of entrance than of exit; and it is but
> common prudence to see our way out before we venture in.'
> Aesop

> 'There's a trick to the Graceful Exit. It begins with the vision
> to recognize when a job, a life stage, a relationship is over –
> and to let go. It means leaving what's over without denying its
> value.' Ellen Goodman

Ideally, your influence will outlive you. In order for that to happen,
however, not only must you have impassioned followers, but the
manner of your leaving must be carefully stage-managed.

Sadly, though, given the amount of time, effort and energy it
takes to achieve influence, it's no wonder that, once secured,
few feel any inclination to relinquish it. Most often, it has to be
wrenched from their grasp. Power is intoxicating, and can confer
on the powerful a sense of immortality – a feeling that the
natural order of waxing and waning need not apply to them.
In the whole of British post-war history, for example, only one
prime minister – Harold Wilson – left office at the time of his

own choosing. The rest went down to ignominious defeat – either at the hands of the electorate or of their own parties. Even the great electoral success stories, Thatcher and Blair, came ultimately to be viewed as liabilities. This is unfortunate, because an unseemly exit can tarnish a great record; the once influential can become defined not so much by their achievements as by personal hubris.

The psychology is interesting. The very self-confidence and perseverance that are essential to becoming truly influential are also the sources of a dangerous self-delusion once success begins to stutter and stagnation or staleness set in. The successful rarely identify themselves as the source of the problem: they've succeeded before; they'll succeed again. One more push should do it, regardless of evidently waning powers or dwindling support.

Picking the right moment to pack it all in, though uncommon, is important in at least two respects. First, you become a yardstick against which your successors will be measured. You want to be a hard act to follow, because that's how the merely influential acquire mythical status. It's possible that you may become even more influential with the passage of time, simply because you left at the top. Your glory days look even better in retrospect. Bill Gates would be a good example; so, too, would Alex Ferguson, the Manchester United boss. Second, you stand much more of a chance of achieving a second or even third act to your career. People like to associate with the powerful; once that power subsides or your reputation becomes tarnished, you are damaged goods, and the invitations swiftly dry up. Ask Fred Goodwin.

MEASURE YOUR OWN PERFORMANCE, OR HAVE PEOPLE AROUND YOU WHO WILL MEASURE IT FOR YOU

The isolating effect of power and positions of influence has already been noted. It can be difficult to find someone willing to tell you the bad news, particularly if it concerns your own performance. That's why smart influencers will ensure that they have in their network colleagues or friends of long standing who can be relied upon to be utterly candid, or who will put in place objective criteria by which their performance can be unarguably measured.

In the field of professional sport, the data is unavoidable and often brutal. You are either scoring goals or you are not. Your lap time is improving or it is not. Your fitness indicators all point to elite levels of performance or they do not. In other realms, the data is often less black and white.

A former CEO told us:

'I always said to my wife, don't let me go on too long. I don't want to be one of those guys who clings on to a position of power even though they are way past their sell-by date. And it's so difficult to judge. But it did happen. We were on holiday one summer, and as the days were counting down to going back home, I just didn't feel that zip anymore. For the first time in my life, I was actually happier doing nothing than contemplating my return to the fray. And my wife looked at me and said, "I think your time's up. You need to move on." And she was right. And I'm glad looking back that I left with my stock pretty high.'

IDENTIFY AND MENTOR YOUR SUCCESSOR EARLY

Early on in your career, rivals are opponents to be neutralized so that they can't do you any damage. Unfortunately, some never lose this sense of paranoia, and never take the trouble to groom their successor. The natural consequence of this negligence is usually grisly. Either the disaffected will rise up and seize the crown from you or the organization does not survive your exit.

A better strategy is to plan for an 'orderly transition' to a hand-picked successor with whom your reputation will be safe. Indeed, a critical moment in the life of the influential comes when they are less concerned with seeking the approbation of senior players and more interested in handing on their own toolkit to juniors.

Succession planning is still the Achilles heel of many organizations, though – even ones with multimillion dollar leadership development processes – suggesting that hubris or inertia are significant impediments to ensuring a long-term legacy.

MOVE ON

The genuinely influential operate in more than one sphere of influence. They can apply their expertise and talent across multiple fields. Thus, when one door closes, several others tend to open. So you should constantly evaluate your options, particularly at times of conspicuous success.

Where will you go next? Where could your expertise and insight take you? Unless you can move on from your main sphere of influence, you are likely to become a hindrance, the dreaded 'back-seat driver', and will do your reputation irreparable damage as a result.

It's perfectly acceptable, of course, to act as a sounding board to your successor, whenever he or she desires it. But this should be a private affair, and you should resist at all costs undermining him or her in public.

Let go, completely. The danger of not doing so is apparent in the story of the founder of a successful recruitment business, who handed over the reins to a highly regarded successor but who, unlike Elvis, most certainly did not leave the building.

'He kept an office, and often used to come in and sit behind his desk, and nobody quite knew what he was doing,' reports a mystified employee. 'And he would drop into meetings unannounced and not say anything but just be there. And eventually, of course, he was challenged, and there was a huge argument and he said, "Of course I've got a right to be here, I put up these four walls, I've got more right to be here than anyone else." And it was sad, this legendary figure just not being able to deal with not being in the thick of it...'

Putting it all together

George Harrison was right: all things must pass. And the sooner you realize that that includes you, the sooner you will be able to plan an exit strategy that allows you dignity and maximum leverage going forward. Knowing that your tenure has a time limit will be energizing. You won't put off till tomorrow what needs to be done today, and the clear identification of a successor will ensure that the transition, when it comes, will be handled smoothly.

But the real benefit will be to you. Actors have only one fear bigger than serial unemployment, and that is typecasting. Tom Baker was a British actor of considerable range and virtuosity, whose early credits included Shakespeare and the National Theatre. The trouble was that, once he became embedded in the nation's consciousness as Doctor Who, the TV role he played with distinction for seven years in the 1970s, he barely worked again. He couldn't transcend the audience stereotype. Maybe if he'd left the programme after three years, at the height of his fame, casting directors would have been more open-minded.

Don't let one influential role define your whole life. Quit at the top, and have the freedom to go and be influential in multiple spheres.

- Do you have a timeframe in mind for your current job, project or assignment?
- Do you know what your next move will be?
- What measures do you have in place to alert you to declining performance?

Have a plan – but keep it quiet

> 'If you don't design your own life plan, chances are you'll fall into someone else's plan. And guess what they have planned for you? Not much.' Jim Rohn

> 'To achieve great things, two things are needed; a plan, and not quite enough time.' Leonard Bernstein

> 'Basically you have to suppress your own ambitions in order to be who you need to be.' Bob Dylan

> 'Always forgive your enemies; nothing annoys them so much.' Oscar Wilde

> 'If you strip away self-effacement, charm and the spirit of mischief – qualities that make determination and ambition tolerable – you're left with a right ***hole.' Russell Brand, *My Booky Wook*

As we have seen, there are many ways in which influence can be secured. It is in the slow accumulation of these tactics over time that enough influence can be won to start to do something meaningful with it. One aspect we have not covered so far, though, is the extent to which influence is arrived at as part of a calculated plan. To what extent should your ambitions be discussed and aired in public?

The responses of my interviewees were pretty consistent on this. They mostly recognized a high need for achievement within themselves early on, and registered in due course that, without influence, it was going to be hard for them to live the life they wanted. Although they aspired to be principals rather than extras, they also realized that their aspirations were best kept private.

Not for nothing does Shakespeare have his version of Julius Caesar refuse the crown three times. Nothing is less likely to assist your pursuit of influence than too obvious a hunger for it. Other people are your biggest obstacle to achieving influence, and it is your management of other people on the way up that to a large extent dictates your chances of reaching the summit.

A CEO described this vividly to us:

'What you have to understand is that, while relatively few people actually want to accept the responsibility of leadership or positions of influence for themselves, most of them sure as hell don't want you to get there either. So you have this huge deadweight of people who just get in your way. And the conundrum is this: until you have reached a position of real influence, you can't do anything about them. To get there, you actually have to work with and through them. And this can wear a lot of talented people out. Don't let the bastards grind you down is fine in principle, but how does it work in practice?'

Three final things to consider on your journey towards influence are to take one step at a time, lead without appearing to lead, and avoid provoking the enemy.

FOCUS ON NO MORE THAN ONE STEP AHEAD

Whether your ultimate ambition is to run a multinational, become President or influence the world through a widely read blog, it is dangerous to concentrate too much on the endgame. See your journey instead as a series of stepping stones and focus your attention on safely negotiating the next step. It is incredibly rare that someone catapults from nowhere into a position of influence – even Barack Obama, whose rise is often portrayed as vertiginous, served seven years as a state senator in Illinois before arriving at the US senate in 2005. Tiresome as it may be, we have to earn our spurs.

Even in the online world, overnight success is unlikely. Most instances of things 'going viral', more often than not, lead to notoriety, not influence. The A-list bloggers I spoke to built their following methodically, first by joining in discussions on other people's blogs, then by seeking the endorsement of existing stars and then by putting great energy into the nurturing of their first few followers.

Make the focus of your attention excelling in your current role, which will provide a bridge to the next clearly defined step. Careless talk about long-term visions is likely to get you a bad name. Delusions of grandeur are not selection criteria for many intermediate management positions.

LEAD WITHOUT APPEARING TO LEAD

All this is not to suggest that you just apply your nose to the grindstone and churn out miscellaneous or meaningless work week after week. In fact, you'll be doing plenty to position yourself for the future, but these tasks will not have a label marked 'wannabe influencer' attached to them. As already discussed, making a wider contribution and implementing change in a non-ostentatious way are two of the best tactics for the gradual accretion of influence.

Give your time willingly and without recompense. Support someone else's initiative. Implement your own ideas and share the credit. Offer suggestions but do it in a self-deprecating way. Help someone out who is below you in the hierarchy, or less experienced. These are all ways of demonstrating leadership and positioning yourself to be influential without screaming naked ambition. They require an upfront investment of time and effort now – and the dividend gets paid out over time. This is, effectively, the 'hairshirt strategy' to making friends and influencing people.

Marco, who runs the regulatory arm of a financial services business, feels he paid his dues:

'When you are in the middle stage of your career, when you are no longer a newbie learning the ropes but you haven't yet acquired any real power or responsibility, that's where you need to put in the time, because people are watching. They are making up their minds about you. Are you a time-server or a value-creator? That's where I did a lot of my mentoring of other people and sitting on discussion groups. Some of it was enjoyable and some of it wasn't, but it helped my profile and creates the right impression. The people who wait to be told to do this stuff often miss the boat.'

AVOID PROVOKING THE ENEMY

The CEO at the start of the chapter talked about the 'deadweight of people who get in your way'. Most of the time this is a pretty supine group – they are the time-servers in an organization. This doesn't mean that they can be disregarded or taken for granted, however. When roused, this population is deadly.

Avoid all talk of aspirations with these people, but stand apart from their gossip and negativity, too. Studied neutrality is the best policy. Having no ambition themselves, they despise it in other people. So when UK politician Michael Heseltine famously traced his desired career path on the back of an envelope as an Oxford student, and wrote 'become Prime Minister' as its culmination, other students who themselves went on to have political careers made it their business from that day on to deny him his wish. They, not he, succeeded.

It's advisable to avoid burning bridges, too. There will be people whose odious views you find intolerable, and the temptation is to tell them so. Embarrass, humiliate or upbraid a certain kind of person in public, and you will have to deal with their enmity for the rest of your career. Good operators are scrupulously polite to opponents in public; the best are not averse to making the occasional flattering comment about them. Keeping opposition contained seems to be the key – and avoiding fanning the flames.

'We don't have to make everyone love us,' one of my interviewees told me. 'But it's reckless to create enemies unnecessarily, particularly if they are lower down the food chain. Hell hath no fury like an administrator scorned.'

Putting it all together

If you find yourself not being heard, or if you have a wish to change the existing order of things, it is as well to plan for acquiring greater influence. But discretion is certainly required as you move up the ladder – you don't want to unleash any forces of negativity that will put obstacles in your way before you reach the top. Ambition is no bad thing except when it rides roughshod over too many opponents.

- What is the 'next step' for you? What do you need to achieve now to progress?
- Where are you investing time and effort over and above the requirements of your job? Where are you leading without seeming to lead?
- How do you handle opponents? Have you made any enemies recently? Could they do you damage in the longer term?

ACKNOWLEDGEMENTS

I would first of all like to thank everyone who agreed to be interviewed for the book. I have the privilege of working with many influential people around the world, and it always astonishes me how generous most of them are with their time and insights.

Huge thanks also to Jess, Freya and Sarah who influence me very effectively on a daily basis!